If These
WALLS
Could TALK:
ST. LOUIS CARDINALS

If These
WALLS
Could TALK:
ST. LOUIS CARDINALS

Stories from the
*St. Louis Cardinals Dugout,
Locker Room, and Press Box*

Stan McNeal

TRIUMPH
BOOKS

No part of this publication may be reproduced, stored in a retrieval system, or transmitted in any form by any means, electronic, mechanical, photocopying, or otherwise, without the prior written permission of the publisher, Triumph Books LLC, 814 North Franklin Street, Chicago, Illinois 60610.

Library of Congress Cataloging-in-Publication Data is available.

This book is available in quantity at special discounts for your group or organization. For further information, contact:

Triumph Books LLC
814 North Franklin Street
Chicago, Illinois 60610
(312) 337–0747
www.triumphbooks.com

Printed in U.S.A.
ISBN: 978-1-62937-053-8
Design by Amy Carter
Photos courtesy of Getty Images

For my parents, Jack and Joyce McNeal.
There's no one I'd rather talk ball with than the Chief.

And to my wife, Colleen. I couldn't have done it without you.

CONTENTS

FOREWORD

Ihave had the pleasure of being a Cardinals fan since birth. And, as someone who grew up rooting for the Cardinals, it has been a unique and unexpected blessing to broadcast their games for the last 18 years. It is both an honor and a great responsibility. Those who came before me are legendary, and Cardinals fans have come to expect the highest level of performance from their broadcast team.

The heightened expectations, of course, go not only to the broadcasters, but also to the entire organization. With that in mind, as a fan my impression was that the Cardinals were one of the organizations that "got it." They honored their tradition, treated their fans with respect, and always competed on the field. That impression has been confirmed now that I am able to peek behind the curtain. The Cardinals do "get it." St. Louis fans should be proud of their organization not just for its winning tradition, but also because it is known throughout the league as one of the true first-class organizations in professional sports.

As any fan of the team knows, we are currently enjoying another Golden Age for the Cardinals. The team is on a sustained run of success that is truly remarkable. Players have changed, the manager has changed, but the success has remained. Team ownership deserves credit for allowing flexibility to improve the team where it makes sense, all the while without mortgaging the future. John Mozeliak and his talented front office team should get a ton of credit for putting the machine in place for this continued success. Mike Matheny deserves credit for taking the mantle from Tony La Russa and not missing a beat. Tony, of course, was instrumental in starting this Golden Age. And, finally, team leaders like Chris Carpenter, Adam Wainwright, Albert Pujols, Jim Edmonds, Yadier Molina, and others deserve credit for maintaining a clubhouse that thrives on professionalism and competition.

Think of the names in that last paragraph. Tony La Russa—Hall of Famer. Albert Pujols—certain Hall of Famer. Jim Edmonds—arguable Hall of Famer. Yadier Molina—on the path to being a Hall of Famer.

Chris Carpenter and Adam Wainwright—two of the most dominant starters of their eras, a Cy Young Award winner and a perennial Cy Young contender. And the roster continues to be stacked with players who can pick up and meet that tradition. As I said earlier, we are in a Golden Age for Cardinals baseball and I honestly do not see an end in sight.

Against that backdrop let me now talk about this book. Stan McNeal "gets it," too. From his vantage point as a journalist covering the team, he has access to the kind of stories that do not make the news accounts of the games. He has taken that access and delivered an eye-opening and revealing account of some of the biggest games and moments of the Cardinals' past few years. This book will not just help you relive some of the great moments of the past few seasons (which are numerous), it also will put those games and moments in a new light for you. You will hear from the key players and coaches about what it was like to be in those games, to play in those moments and you will come away with an even greater appreciation for them, the game, and the organization. You will learn about the game from an insider's perspective, which is why this book is a must-read not only for any Cardinals fan, but also for any fan of the game of baseball.

—Dan McLaughlin
Cardinals play-by-play broadcaster

INTRODUCTION

Bill DeWitt Jr. stood inside the Cardinals clubhouse at Busch Stadium, basking in another celebration. A steady flow of players, coaches and staffers, their family members, media members, and anyone with access to the clubhouse looked to shake hands with and offer congratulations to the chairman of the club.

It's a scene DeWitt has become quite familiar with since he took over the team in 1995, and never more than in the past four years. Since 2011, watching the Cardinals spray champagne has become as much a part of October in St. Louis as trick or treating. The Cardinals have reveled in eight of these postseason parties in the past four years—more than any team in the majors. During that time they have won a World Series, two pennants, and become the first team in the 21st century to make it to a league championship series—the final four of the major leagues—in four consecutive seasons.

Their farm system has been lauded as one of the best in the game, a development that has allowed the Cardinals to maintain a reasonable payroll—by baseball standards, of course—as they enjoy all this winning. No team has won more games in the past four years either. The Detroit Tigers lead the majors in regular season wins since 2011 with one more than the Cardinals, but include the postseason, and St. Louis is No. 1 with an average of a remarkable 99 wins a season.

As I stood in the clubhouse, trying to stay dry, I rattled off some of these superlatives to DeWitt and asked him, "Is this the greatest era in the history of the Cardinals franchise or what?"

He paused, long enough that I started to think my question was so obvious he didn't need to answer. "I'll leave that up to others to decide," he said. "I will say that we have a good thing going and I hope we can keep it going."

I'm not that surprised he didn't answer me more directly. He had no reason to boast and, besides, comparing eras is difficult. But from the smile on DeWitt's face and the twinkle in his eyes, I could tell my question was one he did not mind hearing. And if this isn't the best stretch in franchise history, it has to be "tied for first," as Tony La Russa might say. Lifelong St. Louisan and noted TV announcer Joe Buck, who knows a little about baseball, doesn't remember seeing the Cardinals enjoy a greater run. "I can remember back to the 1970s and I cannot recall a time when they were anywhere close to where they are right now at the major league level and with the guys they keep bringing up," Buck told me in 2014. "They are the envy of baseball—the way they have built this system."

Longtime catcher A.J. Pierzynski, who spent the second half of the 2014 season with the Cardinals after spending 16-plus seasons on other teams, offered the perspective of one who has seen the Cardinals' success from both sides. "It's almost the Cardinals' birthright to get in the playoffs and win a World Series," he says. "It's pretty cool to be a part of."

The Cardinals might have made playing in October seem like part of the club's DNA, but they have endured as many challenges and hardships as any team. They have bid farewell to Hall of Fame manager La Russa and the great slugger Albert Pujols. They've dealt with their share of injures like every team, losing pitching mainstays Chris Carpenter for nearly two years before he retired and Adam Wainwright and Jason Motte for one season each.

Of course, the departure of Pujols has helped the franchise far more than it hurt. The Cardinals wanted to keep him in St. Louis badly enough they made him an offer they probably would have regretted within years. Instead, they have been able to use the savings elsewhere and they turned the compensatory draft pick into the selection of young ace Michael Wacha. "By Albert not coming back, we had resources that we could redeploy elsewhere," general manager John Mozeliak said. "I knew it was going to require a different strategy. Fortunately for us, it has worked. One thing about this organization: when we have to adapt or do an audible, we're able to do so."

It's not just all the winning that has given reason to spoil Cardinals fans. How they have won has been just as exciting. No team in any sport has pulled off as many dramatic victories as the Cardinals in a four-year span. Consider this lineup of thrillers.

- **Game 5 of the 2011 NLDS** Chris Carpenter outduels good friend Roy Halladay, the National League's best pitcher at the time, in a 1–0 complete-game victory against the Philadelphia Phillies to give the Cardinals their first playoff series victory since the 2006 World Series.

- **Game 6 of the 2011 World Series** In what is regarded as one of the greatest World Series games ever, the Cardinals were nine outs from the end and trailed the Texas Rangers by three runs but rallied for an 11–9 victory. Twice the Cardinals were down to their last strike, and twice hometown hero David Freese delivered massively clutch hits, including a walk-off home run in the 11th inning.

- **Game 5 of the 2012 NLDS** They haven't forgotten this one in the nation's capital. The Cardinals trailed 6–0 early and 7–5 entering the ninth at Washington when they rallied for four runs—all recorded with two outs—to pull out a 9–7 victory against the Nationals.

- **Game 3 of the 2013 World Series** In the only Fall Classic game ever decided by a walk-off interference play, Allen Craig rushed home with the winning run after an errant throw to third led to him being tripped. Adding to the drama, Craig was playing with a sore left foot that had kept him out of the lineup for seven weeks before the World Series, inspiring teammate Matt Carpenter to describe his effort as "Gibson-esque."

- **Game 1 of the 2014 NLDS** Trailing Clayton Kershaw and the Dodgers 6–2 in the seventh inning, the Cardinals erupted for eight runs against the game's best pitcher and then held on for a 10–9 victory against Los Angeles. Kershaw had been given a four-run lead 67 times in his career and never lost until Carpenter and Co. got him again.

There have been more than comebacks and shutouts to keep Cardinals Nation on the edge of its collective seat for the past four years. There was Pujols' three-homer show in the World Series, Wacha's breakout October, Matt Carpenter's classic at-bats against Kershaw, La Russa's bullpen-phone snafu in Texas, the wild-card game in Atlanta that turned on an infield-fly call, and much, much more. And that's just the postseason.

No wonder Cardinals fans have gained a reputation in some baseball circles for being spoiled. How could they not be? It's only natural to get a bit greedy when you have witnessed so much history that has gone in your team's favor.

I feel fortunate to have been in St. Louis for this run and I'm not even a Cardinals fan.

As a journalist, I am a fan of good stories, and the Cardinals have provided me no shortage of opportunities. We moved to St. Louis from San Diego in 2000 when I took a job as baseball editor for *The Sporting News*. Since I was named after the greatest Cardinal of them all (Stan the Man), it seemed almost destined. Though I oversaw coverage for all 30 teams, *The Sporting News* was based in St. Louis so Busch Stadium became my office away from the office.

As *The Sporting News* tried (and tried) to re-invent itself, I eventually became a full-time baseball writer. Eventually, the re-inventions caught up to me, and I was laid off the day after I returned from spring training in 2013. Soon enough, I was able to hook on with foxsports.com and now I write about the Cardinals.

I also have raised a son, Jackson, who has to be about as big a Cardinals fan as you will find. My youngest daughter, Kate, can tell you that. Many times she has requested a five-minute, no-Cardinals talk zone at the dinner table. We moved from San Diego to St. Louis before Jackson entered first grade. He had started out a Padres fan. (Yes, they exist.) But it did not take long to switch allegiances. If he had not converted by the end of the 2000 season when the Cardinals won 95 games and the Padres 76, Albert Pujols' arrival in 2001 completed his transformation.

The deal was certainly sealed when the Cardinals played their first game at Busch Stadium following 9/11. We went together that night with no tickets and no sense of what the mood would be like. As we were approaching the stadium, a stranger gave us two tickets that happened to be for seats 20 rows behind the plate. We had a great view when Jack Buck read his poem in tribute to the occasion. I have no idea if the Cardinals won or who they even played, but that really didn't matter that night.

These days we talk more than ever about the Cardinals. When they win, the conversation usually centers on how great a player Yadier Molina, Adam Wainwright, or Lance Lynn is. When they lose, it's often Jackson ripping Mike Matheny and me trying to defend the manager. I don't mind, though. Jackson's complaints prepare me for the others I am likely to hear before the next game. Plus, I honestly believe Matheny has done an excellent job.

I don't expect you to necessarily agree with my take on Matheny, but that's okay. My objective in the chapters ahead was to share as much fascinating, interesting, and inside-the-clubhouse-walls information that I could about the Cardinals and the past four seasons. There certainly were a ton of heroes and victories and celebrations to draw from. I hope you enjoy.

PART I:
2014

Cardinals Record: 90–72

Cardinals Finish: Won NLDS against Los Angeles Dodgers

Beating Kershaw Again

Before Dodgers left-hander Clayton Kershaw threw the pitch, Adam Wainwright predicted what lefty slugger Matt Adams was going to do. "I said, 'If he throws a strike breaking ball right here, he's going to hit a home run,'" Wainwright said. "And he sure did."

And what a home run it was.

Adams' three-run, seventh-inning shot that had been called by Wainwright—teammate John Lackey corroborated the claim—wiped out the Los Angeles Dodgers' 2–0 lead and made the difference in a 3–2 victory that clinched the Cardinals' fourth consecutive trip to the National League Championship Series. The magnitude of the homer was matched only by its implausibility. Consider:

- Kershaw had given up only one homer to a left-handed hitter (Bryce Harper of the Washington Nationals) the entire regular season.
- Adams had struggled mightily against lefties with a .190 batting average against them during the regular season and went without a homer off one for three months.
- Kershaw had faced 1,139 lefty hitters in his career and had never thrown a curveball to one that had resulted in a home run.

No wonder Adams said he was not looking for a breaker after he had fouled off a 93 mph fastball for strike one. "I have it in the back of my mind that he's got a good one, but I'm just looking for a pitch up in the zone," Adams said, "saw it pop out of his hand, and knew it was going to be a good one to swing at."

Adams was talking to me with a beer in one hand and his T-shirt soaked from champagne and beer in the Cardinals' clubhouse celebration. He already had appeared in the postgame interview room, calling it the biggest hit of his young career. Adams, 6'3" and 250 pounds (at

Matt Adams celebrates after hitting a three-run home run against Los Angeles Dodgers pitcher Clayton Kershaw in Game 4 of the 2014 NLDS.

least), had looked like an overgrown kid as he literally skipped around first base. "I don't think I touched the ground the whole way around the bases," he said. About the 386-foot homer that landed in the Cardinals bullpen, Adams said, "I was just looking for a pitch to drive it to the gap to move the guys into scoring position. That's what this team does. We keep the line moving."

As unlikely as was the outcome against Kershaw, no one should have been too surprised. This was not the first time the Cardinals had beaten Kershaw in the postseason. In the past two Octobers, the Cardinals have faced Kershaw four times, and four times they have beaten him. Twice they have beaten Kershaw to end the Dodgers' season. "Just bad déjà vu all over again," Kershaw said. "I can't really put it into words."

Kershaw had lost only three games all season for the Dodgers while winning 21, posting a 1.77 ERA, and taking his reputation as the game's best pitcher to even greater heights. He deservingly won his third NL Cy Young Award in November, and this time it was by a unanimous vote. He became the first pitcher to sign a $200 million contract last January when the Dodgers awarded him a seven-year, $215 million deal that included an $18 million signing bonus.

But he just can't beat St. Louis. The Cardinals have given Kershaw more losses—nine (including the postseason)—than any team in the majors. His 4.13 ERA in 19 starts against the Cardinals is his highest against any National League team. Kershaw was close in these past two postseasons, but one at-bat or one inning made the difference between winning and going home.

In Game 2 of last year's NLCS, the Cardinals beat Kershaw 1–0 on an unearned run. Third baseman David Freese led off the bottom of the fifth with a double and advanced to third when Dodgers catcher A.J. Ellis did not catch a routine pitch. "Fastball right down the middle, I just missed it," he told reporters. Adding to the Dodgers' frustration, Freese scored on a sacrifice fly by Jon Jay that came one pitch after he had fouled back an attempt to bunt home the run. "You're not going to get a lot of chances against the best pitcher in the league," Freese said. "Even though you lead off with a double, it doesn't give you a good chance of scoring off a guy like that. We were fortunate that Jon Jay…battled back and hit a tough pitch."

Six days later in Game 6, with the Cardinals needing one win to advance to the World Series, Matt Carpenter cracked Kershaw in a confrontation that won't be forgotten by either side. It took 11 pitches before Carpenter delivered a one-out double that changed the game. He fouled off five straight two-strike pitches. In one sequence he fouled off a fastball, curve, and slider as Kershaw tried everything he had to retire the lefty-hitting leadoff man. But then, after three straight fastballs, Kershaw left a slider too far up, and Carpenter lined it into right field. "Every pitch I fouled off, the crowd got louder and louder," Carpenter recalled after the game. "That sharpened my focus. I know he's the best pitcher in baseball and I know he's not going to give in either. I was just trying not to strike out. He struck me out the first at-bat and got ahead of me again. I was like, *I'm not striking out. I'm putting this ball in play somehow.* I just kept trying to stay short and foul pitches off. I was able to do it."

Dodgers manager Don Mattingly explained what happened next. "The floodgates opened," he said. Carlos Beltran singled on a ball that deflected off second baseman Mark Ellis' glove to score Carpenter with the Cardinals' first run. After Matt Holliday was called out on strikes for the second out, the Cardinals went single, single, walk, and single. Kershaw threw 48 pitches in the inning, and the Cardinals took a 4–0 lead. They blew open the game in their half of the fifth inning with two singles and a double by Adams that chased Kershaw. The final was 9–0.

In Game 1 of the 2014 National League Division Series, Kershaw started against Wainwright at Dodger Stadium in what was billed as the pitcher's duel of the postseason. Wainwright, who also won 20 games, had been named by manager Mike Matheny to start the All-Star Game, and the decision drew criticism from some on the West Coast who felt Kershaw was more deserving.

This time Kershaw looked like he would conquer the Cardinals, though he gave up a home run to the second batter he faced, rookie Randal Grichuk. He then set down the next 16 Cardinals before allowing a homer to Carpenter with two out in the sixth. With Wainwright struggling, Kershaw carried a 6–2 lead into the seventh. At this point in his seven-year career, that meant a guaranteed victory. According to the Dodgers, Kershaw had been given that large a lead 67 times and never had lost.

Leave it to the Cardinals to change that.

Kershaw had been efficient with his pitches and entered the seventh having thrown 81. But on a hot, 90-degree day, he lost his effectiveness in a hurry. Kershaw's inning went like this: Holliday led off with a

5

line-drive single up the middle, Jhonny Peralta followed with a line-drive single up the middle, and Yadier Molina loaded the bases with a ground-ball single up the middle.

Adams then lined a single—again up the middle—to make the score 6–3 with the bases still loaded. All these hits to center field were not a coincidence either. The preferred approach of Cardinals hitters is to take the ball up the middle. Pete Kozma struck out for the first out before Jay singled in a run to left to make it 6–4 with the bases still loaded. Pinch-hitter Oscar Taveras then struck out, and Kershaw was just one out away from escaping with the Dodgers' lead in tact.

But then came the big hit again provided by Carpenter. This time, on pitch No. 8, he slammed a bases-cleaning double off the right-field fence that missed being a grand slam by only a few feet. The Cardinals led 7–6, and Kershaw, mercifully, was headed to the showers. "There was a moment during that at-bat where I was feeling kind of the same emotions I was having last year," Carpenter said. "It was a very similar at-bat. I was just being competitive and really having a tough AB and, in an inning where we had a lot of action, I was just trying to keep the line moving. I was able to get a pitch that I could handle and something I could put the barrel on. I hit it in the gap and ended up being a big play for us."

Neither team was done scoring, though, and the Cardinals hung on for a 10–9 victory that ended with the tying run on third.

Undeterred by Kershaw's lack of success against St. Louis, Mattingly started his ace on three days' rest when the Dodgers faced elimination in Game 4 at Busch Stadium. Again, Kershaw dominated the Cardinals early. He had allowed only three base runners through six innings and, after the Dodgers took a 2–0 lead in the top of the sixth, showed no signs of tiring. He struck out Kozma, Carpenter, and Grichuk in the St. Louis side of the sixth.

But the seventh inning again proved his undoing. Holliday started the inning with a ground single that barely eluded second baseman

Dee Gordon, and Jhonny Peralta followed with a single that shortstop Hanley Ramirez managed to put a glove on but could not stop. Kershaw then hung an 0–1 curve to Adams for his decisive home run, a line drive that initially looked like it might not land over the fence. "I saw [Matt] Kemp tracking it really well," Matheny said. "It looked like he was right on it. I thought this could be caught. Then, when it cleared the fence, I did pretty much what 45,000 other people did."

Wong Flips Out

The first time Kolten Wong looked like he was ready to take over second base for the Cardinals was March 7, 2014, in Port St. Lucie, Florida, spring home of the New York Mets. After a rough first week in spring training, Wong showed off his all-around game by collecting three hits, stealing a base, and making two strong defensive plays. "It's about time," he said. "It's a weight off my chest."

Four days later the young Hawaiian turned in an even more impressive performance long before he homered in that day's exhibition. As the Cardinals gathered in the outfield for their early morning stretching at Roger Dean Stadium, Wong brought everyone to a standstill when, from a standing position, he flipped over backward and landed on his feet as smoothly as a trained gymnast.

Not far from where the players were warming up, manager Mike Matheny was holding court with reporters at the time. The Cardinals manager happened to be answering a question about Wong when he stopped in mid-sentence. "Did you guys see that?" He asked, clearly impressed. None of us had, but right about then, Wong repeated the feat for anyone who had not been watching.

As much as the acrobatics said about his athleticism, the back-flip said more about Wong's mental state. After a month in camp, he finally appeared comfortable enough to have a little fun. Matheny and his teammates had been reminding Wong to enjoy the journey, but he was too focused on trying to prove himself. "It's a great step for him," Matheny said. "He wears stuff hard. It's the kind of player he is. He'll evolve over time. Typically, a little success frees you up."

Matheny already had met with Wong in an attempt to help him relax. After a talk with his manager as well as a few hits, something finally seemed to be clicking. "I'm confident in myself that I can play at this level," Wong said. "I'm understanding that and buying into it."

He considers his backflipping to be no big deal. Wong said he was just proving his gymnastic skills to a couple of teammates who had doubted him. He learned the move when he was at the University of Hawaii and frequented a gymnastics facility with his now fiancée. "I can almost do it on command," he shrugged. "I'm that confident with it."

He was not ready to tread on hallowed Cardinals history, though, and mimic the entrance made famous by Hall of Famer Ozzie Smith. Wong had yet to master the "Ozzie flip." "That cartwheel to the backflip I've tried," he said. "I can't land straight. It's the hardest thing."

Wong soon would find something even more difficult to handle than a flip: his rookie season in the major leagues. Wong experienced enough ups and downs in his first full season as a big leaguer that at times he felt like he was on a non-stop loop of backflips. He struggled mightily at the outset of spring training but ended up leading the team in hitting in March. Then he started the regular season slowly and before April was over was sent to the minors. He returned and went on a run that earned him National League Rookie of the Month for May. June wasn't a week old before he bruised his left shoulder and eventually landed on the disabled list. When he came off the disabled list, he went off again, hitting five homers in seven games.

And that was just the first half.

A game against the Boston Red Sox on August 7 typified the emotional roller coaster that was Wong's 2014. He hit two homers and scored a third run to lead the Cardinals to a 5–2 victory. At the same time, updates from home were coming in about a pair of hurricanes heading at Hilo, Hawaii. "It sucks not being able to be there," Wong said. By the end of the day, as Hilo avoided any major damage, the folks back home were having a little fun at his expense. "My friends were texting me, telling me that the winds from there came here and blew my hits out," Wong said. "Thanks guys, I appreciate it. I guess I don't have any pop."

That Wong was able to joke around with the media showed just how far he had come. He had faced one difficulty after another almost since he had been promoted for the first time less than a year earlier. He took his shortcomings to heart, too. Within hours after he had been embarrassingly picked off to end Game 4 of the 2013 World Series, Wong took to Twitter to apologize to Cardinals fans.

Nothing had been as hard about the past year as losing his mom, Keala Wong, to a long battle with cancer. Wong was home for the offseason when she died six days before Christmas. "She was always the one with me, the one I would call when times got tough," Wong told *West Hawaii Today*. "Now, I'm doing this for her to keep it going. Anybody who played with me or against me knew she was the loudest on the field, always cheering. She's the one who would keep me even-keeled, relaxed, not getting too high or too low. She had a love for her kids and always wanted us to be successful. That support is the biggest thing. She was always there for us. My favorite memory is growing up and her being my No. 1 fan and having her there at all times."

Wong reported to Florida with a tattoo covering his right arm as a way to remember his mom. He had it put on his right arm because that was his strongest arm. Keala Wong undoubtedly would have been proud at how her oldest son handled his rookie season, which ended in defeat for the Cardinals but still as a success for their young second baseman.

Wong finished the postseason with seven hits—none of them measly singles, either. Three homers, three doubles, and a triple gave him

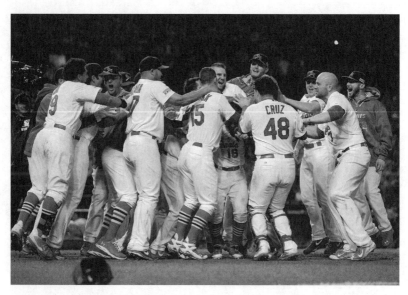

Teammates envelop Kolten Wong (No. 16) after his walk-off home run wins Game 2 of the 2014 NLCS against the San Francisco Giants.

more extra base hits in a single postseason than any National League rookie since Chipper Jones in 1995. And Jones needed more than twice as many plate appearances to beat Wong by one extra-base hit. Wong blasted game-winning home runs in both Game 3 of the National League Division Series and Game 2 of the National League Championship Series. Against the Los Angeles Dodgers, he hit a two-run shot in the seventh inning that broke a 1–1 tie in a game the Cardinals won 3–1.

He slugged an even more dramatic homer came against Sergio Romo and the San Francisco Giants. The Cardinals already were down a game in the best-of-seven series, and, after Trevor Rosenthal blew a one-run lead in the top of the ninth, were three outs from going into extra innings. Busch Stadium had gone silent when Wong led off the bottom of the ninth, but he quickly changed that. Romo threw an 0–1 slider, and Wong lined it into the right-field seats, sending the sold out crowd and his teammates into a frenzy. He had barely crossed the plate before his jersey had been ripped off and shredded into several pieces.

Once a little order had been restored, Wong went looking for backup catcher A.J. Pierzynski, who had volunteered a bit of advice before the at-bat. "Base-hit swing, base-hit swing," Pierzynski had suggested, knowing that Wong sometimes showed a tendency to swing from the heels. Wong looked at his teammate, 14 years his senior, and said, "Was that good enough for you?"

Kelly Leaves and Then Comes Back Quickly

Joe Kelly became a fan favorite in St. Louis for his personality as much as his pitching. He's the guy who dressed up like a very old man and startled the hip-hop superstar Nelly during an interview in the Cardinals dugout. He's the guy known to go on Twitter seeking gamers for late-night Call of Duty action. He's the guy who engaged in a national anthem "stand-off" with a player on the other team before a playoff game.

And yes, he's the guy with the 98 mph fastball that rescued the Cardinals rotation in the second half of 2013. Growing up in Southern California, Kelly was the kid who showed great athleticism but had trouble being noticed because he was undersized. He finally grew so weary of being overlooked by college recruiters and scouts that he devised a scheme to be noticed that only a self-confessed goofball with a bazooka arm could pull off.

When he was attending a showcase event before his senior year at Corona High, Kelly decided that when the ball came to him during practice, he would try to throw it to the four-story dormitory that stood across the street from the third-base dugout. He was stationed in right field. "I was messing with my buddy and said, 'Hey, I bet you I can throw a line drive right off that building,'" Kelly said. "He's like, do it. I was a goofball. So okay, I'm going to do it on the first throw."

Sure enough, when the ball came to Kelly, he fielded it and promptly threw it over the cutoff man, airmailed the dugout, and smacked the building. His mission to be noticed was accomplished. "When he threw that one halfway up the building, it really stood out," said Andrew Checketts, who soon would become Kelly's pitching coach at University of California Riverside. "I remember going back to my boss and telling him about this kid with as good an arm as another outfielder who was considered to have one of the best arms in Southern California. My boss said, 'Yeah right. There's no way.'"

But within days, UC Riverside coach Doug Smith had Kelly on campus. "On the spot they offered me books and tuition scholarship," Kelly said. "I was like, all right, I'm in." Kelly went to college as an outfielder but ended up as Riverside's closer and soon was attracting the attention of the pro scouts. The Cardinals took him in the third round of the 2009 draft, and three years later, he reached St. Louis.

With the Cardinals, Kelly became as well-liked by his teammates as by fans, which resulted in many tears being shed in the clubhouse on July 31, 2014, when he, along with Allen Craig, was traded to the Boston Red Sox for John Lackey. Both Kelly and Craig had become core members of the Cardinals, and, while neither was enjoying a very good season, the trade still surprised just about everyone.

One of the most stunned Cardinals was fellow starter Shelby Miller, Kelly's best friend. Miller had been Kelly's best man at his wedding in November 2013, just weeks after Kelly had served as a groomsman at Miller's wedding. On the day of the deal, Miller was clearly shaken and not only because his buddy was leaving. He realized he could have been the one who had been sent packing, something that happened during the 2014 offseason.

In a twist that only the schedule-makers could provide, Miller would not have to wait long to see Kelly again. The Red Sox were visiting Busch Stadium the very next week, and in another scheduling quirk, Kelly's first start for his new team would be made against his previous team—and his best bud. Since they would be matched up in the second game of the series, Kelly could spend time before the first game checking in with his just-departed teammates. He already had a story to tell them after spending his first weekend in Boston. Because he had not been put on the 25-man roster until Saturday, he attended Friday night's game against the New York Yankees as a fan. He used his Players Association pass, scored a seat five rows behind home plate, and even Tweeted out a photo of Derek Jeter in the on-deck circle. "I yelled at Jeter a few times, just trying to be a fan, called him a bum," Kelly said. "No, I'm just kidding. I would never do that. But it was fun to see a game like that."

Miller and Kelly had communicated mostly by text since the trade, but they were able to share a hug before the series opener on Tuesday. Kelly had more than that on his mind, too. He wanted to raise the stakes for Wednesday night. "He said if he gets a hit off me, I owe him 100 bucks and vice versa," Miller said. Still, Kelly said his goal for pitching to Miller would be simple: "Try not to hit him." Added Miller, "It'll be fun, but at the same time, we both know what our job is when it comes down to it. We both want to win and do our best."

They might have tried to treat the night as they would any other start, but Kelly quickly learned it would be different. On his way to the bullpen to warm up, he was showered with applause. The first time he went to the mound, a louder cheer erupted. When he stepped into the on-deck circle before his first at-bat, he received more love from the crowd of 42,733. When he batted for the first time, a standing ovation ensued. Every time he turned around, it seemed Cardinals fans were wishing him well. "That was crazy," Kelly said, "definitely hard to put in words, incredibly awesome. My heart started beating fast, and I just tried to keep it together."

Both of the hard-throwing right-handers did themselves proud with their pitching. They almost matched each others' stat lines with both going seven innings and allowing only one run. Kelly allowed three hits, and Miller gave up four, including one that would cost him the wager. In his first at-bat, Kelly beat out a slow roller to shortstop. The play initially was called an out, but the Red Sox won a replay challenge, giving Kelly an infield single. "I've never seen him run those out like that," Miller said. "He wanted it bad."

Well, Kelly had run that fast at least once before—in April when he ended up tearing his left hamstring and missing the next three months. He admitted that came into his mind when he was sprinting to first. When the game was over, you could hear a sense of relief from both friends in the postgame clubhouses. "There were some emotions," Kelly said. "After that first inning, basically after the first pitch, I realized it was just pitching again. Like pitching in the playoffs, you get really anxious and excited, but once you let go of the ball, it's just pitching again." Said Miller: "I thought it would be maybe a little bit more odd than it was. You don't try to make too much of it. When all that's said and done, you can talk about it. He pitched great, kept our offense a little off-balance. I wish we could have won."

As midnight approached and Busch Stadium was almost empty except for the cleanup crew, Miller wrapped up his interviews and went onto the field to hook up with Kelly. He had to wait a few minutes before Kelly completed his media obligations and hustled out to join him. Both players donned their respective jerseys and, with their wives at their sides, had their photographs taken. This would be a night they remembered. Kelly then headed back to the Red Sox clubhouse, collected his belongings, and continued on with his new life.

Jay the DJ

In most major league clubhouses, that day's starting pitcher typically controls the choice of music—but not on the Cardinals. Center fielder Jon Jay has served as the Cardinals' DJ for the past three years. Reliever

Randy Choate was responsible for the fancy new portable speaker system that appeared in the clubhouse halfway through the 2014 season, but that didn't give him the right to spin the tunes. Song selection remained Jay's domain.

Jay plugs his mobile phone into the stereo, opens the Pandora Radio app, picks a genre, and goes about his business of preparing for that day's game. Hip-hop and rap top his favorites list, but Jay says he's a fan of all types of music. When Georgia native Adam Wainwright is starting, for example, Jay turns on country. Most days, though, Jay leans toward whatever is popular among the 20-somethings at the moment. Or, as 40-something manager Mike Matheny calls the type of music, "awful." He usually says so with a smile, like the old codger who can't believe the younger generation actually listens to such stuff. But you can be sure Eminem hasn't been downloaded to the iPad he keeps on his office desk.

Matheny might not be much of a fan of Jay's musical choices, but there is no bigger backer of Jay's baseball game. On the day the Cardinals traded for Peter Bourjos in November 2013, with the stated implication that he would be taking over center field, Matheny called Jay and assured him that he would not be overlooked. The gesture was one that was appreciated but deemed unnecessary by the man on the other end of the call. "It shows how this organization is willing to do whatever it takes to win," Jay said. "Things are going to happen sometimes that you might not be in favor of individually, but it's a class act when you can have a conversation. That's something that you respect."

Jay pointed out this had not been the first time he had received such a call. After the 2010 season, when Colby Rasmus still was manning center field, the Cardinals signed Lance Berkman to play right field, and left Jay without a starting job. In 2011 Rasmus was traded in part because the club preferred Jay in center field, and the Cardinals went on to win the World Series. Still, after the season the club brought aboard Carlos Beltran to play right field, but with the idea that he could spell Jay to ensure Allen Craig and Matt Adams received ample opportunities to play. In his two years with the Cardinals, however, Beltran played in center only nine times.

Beltran would have received a lot of action in center in 2013 because Jay's production declined, but stress on Beltran's aging knees kept him in right. Jay hit a career-low .276 and struck out a career-high 103 times, but even more concerning to the club was the regression of his outfield play. Shortly after the Cardinals lost to the Boston Red Sox in the 2013 World Series, general manager John Mozeliak said finding an upgrade in center field would be one of his top offseason priorities. Three weeks later the Cardinals landed Bourjos, and Mozeliak all but proclaimed him the Opening Day center fielder.

When Matheny reached out to assure Jay he still would get his chance, the manager heard the same script Jay gave him after the Berkman and Beltran acquisitions. Jay explained his thinking to me later in the season. "I'm here to compete, I'm here to help the team win," he said. "My goal in the beginning of every year is to be playing a lot in September leading into October. I know that to be in the lineup at that point I must have done something during the year."

Jay said this the day before starting in center field and batting second in the first game of the National League Championship Series. Once again, he had responded to the threat of losing playing time by elevating his game throughout the regular season. He finished with a team-best .303 batting average to go with a .372 on-base percentage and, just as importantly, his defense was back to the standards of his first two seasons. "It was different for him this year," Matheny said late in the 2014 season. "But to his credit, I can't think of one day all season when he didn't say, 'Hey, whatever you need me to do, I'll be ready.' And it was sincere. It was nice to see a guy like that take off and prove it to everybody."

Jay might finally have convinced the front office that finding a better fit in center field isn't happening, at least not in the near future. Mozeliak admitted after the 2014 season that Jay's second half had changed how the club views him as a player. "Center field right now is Jon Jay's," Mozeliak said.

As Jay was playing his way back into the club's good graces in 2014, he also was securing a lofty place in Cardinals history. He will enter 2015 tied for fourth all-time on the club in playoff games played. More impressively, he is the only player to have appeared in all 57 playoff games in the Cardinals' four-year run of reaching the NLCS. Succeeding in October and securing a spot in club lore is what Jay is about. "You want to be part of that legacy, part of that Cardinals history," he said. "We see it when guys come into town for reunions of the World Series [winners]. That's a cool thing you point out to a young guy. Hey man, that should be us one day. Twenty years from now when we're old with our families, we'll be coming back to St. Louis to celebrate a world championship. That's what it's about."

Once the young guy being mentored by the likes of Albert Pujols, Chris Carpenter, and Berkman, Jay has emerged as one of the veterans, complete with the postseason experience. "There's a kind of attitude that guys have around here that they pass on to the younger guys," Jay said. "I got so much information and support and advice from guys before, from Albert, Carp, Lance Berkman, Carlos Beltran. I feel like it's my turn now to share that with the younger guys. It's a fun process. Everyday I thank God for this opportunity I've been given."

The son of Cuban immigrants who grew up in Miami, Jay has made as much of his abilities as any player on the roster. He lacks the power of a Kolten Wong, the speed of Bourjos, and the arm of Randal Grichuk, but he finds a way to get the job done. Look at his on-base percentage, which was helped considerably by all the times Jay was hit by pitches. He led the majors in taking one for the team in 2014, with 20 HBPs, and he ranks second over the past four years, with 56.

After virtually every one, Jay calmly drops his bat, lowers his gaze, and trots to first base. No charging the mound, no glaring at the pitcher, no whining to the umpire. It's like he doesn't want to give the pitcher the satisfaction of thinking his fastball can even bruise Jay. "It always hurts, but it's just part of the game," he said. "It's not a big deal to me. It's not like I'm trying to go up there and get hit by a pitch."

Jay stands close to the plate when he steps into the left-handed side of the box and, because pitchers try to work him low and in, he knows he is susceptible to being hit. If it means getting on base, he's only going to try so hard to get out of the way. Clearly, he can play with pain. Jay played much of the second half of the 2014 season with a left wrist so sore that he required offseason surgery. If Matheny had not mentioned the pain to the media, no one outside the trainer's room would have known Jay was hurting. The clubhouse DJ is that quiet when it comes to talking about his game.

The Edge of A.J.

Less than 24 hours after A.J. Pierzynski signed with the Cardinals on July 25, he was catching and batting sixth in a game against the Chicago Cubs. He was booed loud and long all afternoon at Wrigley Field, too.

Of course he was.

He always is.

Cubs fans remember Pierzynski when he was with the Chicago White Sox and bowled over Mike Barrett, instigating a full-blown mess. But with Pierzynski it's always something. He has been considered one of baseball's most annoying players for at least the past 10 years. Whether he's giving hitters an earful as they're trying to hit or "accidentally" stepping on a first baseman's foot trying to beat out a hit or barking pleasantries from the dugout, Pierzynski always has displayed an uncanny ability to rankle opponents. He's even been known to irritate his own teammates more than a time or two.

When major leaguers are polled on the player they'd most like to see take a fastball to the ribs, Pierzynski usually tops the list or is right behind Alex Rodriguez. Pierzynski's reputation as a troublemaker has spread so much that he no longer cares what others think. That is, if he ever did. "It's gotten to a point where everyone just laughs about it," Pierzynski said. "What can you say? There's nothing I can do."

When the Cardinals needed a replacement after Yadier Molina tore up his right thumb, Pierzynski was not considered much of a fill-in candidate because of his reputation. The Red Sox had dumped him earlier in the month, and within days anonymous sources in Boston were ripping him for being a lousy teammate. Surely, the Cardinals wouldn't risk upsetting their clubhouse chemistry by bringing in a veteran that few on the team knew. Pierzynski was still a good player at 37, but he wasn't that good. General manager John Mozeliak, however, decided to give Pierzynski a chance mainly because of his bat, and the club cut ties with George Kottaras, a backup they'd brought in just days after Molina was injured. "I was cautious," Mozeliak said. "We have a very tight clubhouse, and I didn't want to have something that would become disruptive."

Score one for the GM. The only trouble Pierzynski caused in his short time with the Cardinals was to the opposition. He performed as well as expected on the field and injected a welcomed dose of personality into the clubhouse. When Molina returned earlier than expected and Pierzynski was buried on the bench, he did not gripe. When he did not make the roster for the National League Division Series, he did not grumble. "If I'm here, I'm all in for the team to win, whether I was active or not," he said. "I still talked to the guys. I still had guys coming up to me asking questions. At no point did I ever feel I wasn't a part of it."

He had only one encounter with an opponent, and that hardly was his fault. Pierzynski was on his way back to the dugout after making the final out in a loss at Milwaukee when Brewers closer Francisco Rodriguez turned and yelled at him. Though Rodriguez did not explain his displeasure, the Cardinals deduced that the Brewers pitcher felt Pierzynski ran too close to him as he exited the field. Several players from both teams rushed onto the field, but the incident quickly passed. In the visitors' clubhouse afterward, Pierzynski professed innocence and ignorance as to what had happened. On his way from the showers to his locker, he stopped by Mike Matheny's office, raised his arms over his head in apparent exasperation, and said, "I don't know what I did." When I mentioned to Pierzynski that perhaps this was a case when his reputation had preceded him, he said, "I'm sure it does." He added, "Trust me, if it was a few years ago, I probably would have said something."

Pierzynski's mouth undoubtedly at times has overshadowed his accomplishments on the field. Over his 17 seasons in the majors, he's third in hits and RBIs among catchers and owns a .281 batting average. He also is the only catcher in history to log at least 110 games behind the plate for 13 consecutive seasons. Pierzynski spent 13 seasons in the majors before landing on the disabled list with a broken left wrist in 2011. "I was on the DL 15 days, came back, and played the last month with a broken wrist," said Pierzynski, then with the Chicago White Sox. "I probably shouldn't have, but we were in the playoff hunt and I wanted to play."

With the Texas Rangers in 2013, he says he played two weeks with a torn oblique before the team disabled him for the only other time in his career. Again, he stayed on the minimum 15 days. "I don't want to sound like I'm tooting my horn," he said. "But there's been plenty of times when I've been banged up, and you just say, 'Hey, I'm going out there no matter what. It's a lot of want-to.'"

Somehow he escaped two afflictions that often compromise catchers—sore knees and concussions. He figures he's suffered a concussion at some point in his career, but he couldn't tell you when. "I wouldn't even know what one was," he said. "I was talking to [catcher] David Ross in Boston and I'm like, 'How did you know when you had a concussion?'

"'Because things were off,' he said. I've never been to that point where I felt different. I've never had a headache, never felt nauseous, never been in that position. Guys get them from foul tips, and I've been hit by a million foul tips, so somewhere along the way, I'm bound to have had one."

Pierzynski never has tried another position—not even as a kid growing up in Florida. He did, though, play another role with the Cardinals. When Molina returned, Pierzynski became the loudest cheerleader in the dugout. "He's not afraid to yell at people," Matheny said. "He enjoys the competition and he's just going to say whatever comes to his mind. That's who he's always been."

Silent George Returns to St. Louis

Interleague play brought an old teammate to Busch Stadium on July 22, 2014. When he visited, George Hendrick stayed true to his nickname—Silent George. Hendrick stuck to personal policy and did not talk to the media, but he was happy to chat with any of his teammates from the 1980s Cardinals. As Ozzie Smith will tell you, Hendrick hardly was quiet in the clubhouse. "George did not talk to the press, but he was the opposite in the clubhouse," Smith told me shortly before Hendrick came to St. Louis with the Tampa Bay Rays, for whom he serves as the first-base coach. "He was the troublemaker that always kept something going. He was not Silent George to us."

Yet Hendrick could be mysterious around his teammates. Before the Cardinals took the field for the seventh game of the 1982 World Series, Hendrick told his teammates that—win or lose—they should not look for him in any postgame gatherings. "Boys, I'm going to say my goodbyes right now," he told his teammates, according to Smith.

Sure enough, after Hendrick drove in the go-ahead run during a three-run sixth-inning comeback, and the Cardinals went on to beat the Milwaukee Brewers 6–3, he headed to his Porsche and, still in uniform, drove home. To this day, the center fielder on that team, Willie McGee, says that remains his No. 1 memory of the '82 World Series. Some said that Hendrick simply did not want to be bothered. Others said that an illness in the family required his attention more than a World Series celebration. Hendrick, of course, did not say. All these years later, he's still not talking to the press.

Hendrick played 18 seasons in the majors and, except for the first two, he did not speak on the record except for an occasional interview with the *St. Louis Post-Dispatch*'s respected beat writer, Rick Hummel. As a coach and staffer with the Rays since 2006, Hendrick hasn't changed his ways. His silence might have overshadowed a distinguished playing career. Hendrick played for World Series champions in St. Louis and Oakland, made four All-Star teams, and hit .300 in four different seasons. Born and raised in Los Angeles, he was the first pick of the January 1968 draft by the Oakland A's and reached the majors when he was 21. He was traded twice before he came to the Cardinals from San Diego in exchange for lefty starter Eric Rasmussen early in the 1978 season. Hendrick quickly became a mainstay in the Cardinals outfield and would be for the next seven seasons, leading the club in homers and RBIs while hitting .294 during his St. Louis tenure. He was 35 and on the downhill side of his career when he was dealt to the Pittsburgh Pirates before the 1985 season.

Hendrick is also largely credited with leaving a mark on baseball fashion that remains popular 30 years later. In an effort to be more comfortable as the game turned to polyester, Hendrick is considered among the first to wear long, baggy uniform pants down to his shoes.

But Hendrick is known best for what he didn't do: talk to the press. Because he never has set the record straight, no one but him knows exactly why he cut off the media. For his first two seasons in the majors, however, with the Oakland A's in 1971–72, Hendrick was as quotable as the next player. But something changed after he was traded to the Cleveland

Indians before the 1973 season. As one story goes, some veterans on the Indians thought the upstart Hendrick was talking too much about himself, and when word reached him about this, he simply went silent.

But in another, more widely believed version, Hendrick stopped talking after he was burned by a reporter. Early in his first season with the Indians, he hit a winning home run off a pitcher whom he considered a good friend. When talking with reporters after the game, Hendrick offered his opinion that the pitcher should not have been in the game at that point. He had been pitching a lot lately and was worn down.

In the next day's newspapers, the story somehow was twisted. Instead of coming across as defending the pitcher, Hendrick was implicated in saying the pitcher did not belong in the major leagues. He was mortified. Hendrick reported to the ballpark early the next day and planted himself outside the opposing team's clubhouse. As soon as his friend arrived, Hendrick told him that he had been misquoted.

He added that he never would talk to the media again.

Forty-one years later, he rarely has—on the record—to anyone except Hummel. When Hendrick felt like Cardinals fans needed to know what was going on with him, such as when he worked at first base during one spring training, he would grant Hummel an interview. Other times he spoke with his bat. On June 7, 1983, Steve Carlton was facing the Cardinals needing five strikeouts to pass Nolan Ryan and become baseball's all-time strikeout leader. Before the game, Hendrick pulled Hummel aside and matter-of-factly told him there was no way he would be the victim that put Carlton in the record book.

In his first at-bat, Hendrick blasted a two-run homer into the upper deck at Veterans Stadium. Carlton would get the record that day against McGee, but Hendrick's home run made the difference in a 2–1 outcome. After the game Hendrick saw Hummel in the clubhouse and gave him an "I told you so" nod—but no interview. "You're a man of your word," Hummel told him.

Neshek's Number

When Pat Neshek called his mom last August to tell her that he had added Babe Ruth's autograph to his collection, she was not pleased. "She hung up on me," Neshek said.

Evidently baseball moms can be superstitious, too. Paula Neshek was concerned about the price her eldest son had paid for the signed baseball, even though it had not cost him a penny.

But Neshek had given up something that his mom considered quite valuable. He turned over his jersey No. 41 to new teammate John Lackey, who had worn the number for virtually his entire 12-year career. Paula Neshek, for good reason, did not want Pat to change anything. He was enjoying the best season of his career. Why mess with success?

Jersey numbers, though, never had been a big deal to Neshek. Since reaching the majors in 2006, he had worn 72, 17, 34, 40, and 47 before taking 41 when he signed with the Cardinals last winter. Collecting autographs and memorabilia, however, has long been a passion for the veteran reliever. To score a nice addition for his collection would be worth switching numbers.

Negotiations began before Lackey even met his new teammates. He was in Boston when he was traded on July 31 while the Cardinals were finishing a series in San Diego. Lackey would meet the team the next day at Busch Stadium. Somewhere on the return flight to St. Louis, Matt Holliday stepped in to broker the deal. "I think he was getting tired of hearing about it," Neshek said.

Lackey initially offered to buy Neshek a nice watch, the standard gift that a well-compensated veteran would give to keep his number. But Neshek doesn't care much about expensive watches. "I'm kind of into baseball cards," he told Lackey.

Lackey replied: "Go pick one out."

Neshek consulted with a friend in the collectible business and was told to go for a Ruth baseball. Neshek went on eBay, identified some possibilities, and had his buddy check them out. Lackey gave him the okay on one, and Neshek handled the arrangements and the authentication. The one he chose was special even by the Babe's standards. Ruth had put quotation marks around "Babe," which a collectibles expert, such as Neshek, realized made the ball even more valuable. Most of the balls that Neshek had checked did not have the quote marks, which Ruth stopped using later in his career. "A lot of the ones you see are toward the end of his life and career," Neshek said. "This one is from 1926. That was the cool thing about this one. It was during his playing days."

When the ball arrived in the Cardinals clubhouse, Neshek showed it off like a proud owner of a priceless present. Against the advice of some teammates, he took it from its case and went around the lockers. "Look at this, guys," he said. "You want to touch it? It was pretty cool."

Neshek immediately ranked the Ruth ball No. 1 in a collection that includes a note card signed by Jimi Hendrix and a battle plan with Napoleon Bonaparte's signature that was hundreds of years old. The price that Lackey paid remained a secret, but sports memorabilia experts placed the ball's value at no less than $25,000. Lackey shrugged at the cost. "Everything is relative, I guess," he said. "I've done okay in this game and I appreciate him giving up that number with him having such a great year. I wanted to do something cool for him, and he was really happy with it."

Scoring the Ruth autograph was one of the many reasons that Neshek seemed to always be smiling in 2014. He had a year to remember on as well as off the field, a feat made more impressive by how it started. Neshek had spent the previous two seasons with the Oakland A's, but after a so-so 2013, they let him become a free agent. But his phone barely rang in the offseason, and two weeks before training camps opened, Neshek still was looking for a job. "You think, *What the hell had happened?*" Neshek said.

The Cardinals featured a bullpen stocked with young power arms that had blossomed during the 2013 postseason. Still, they were seeking an experienced hand as insurance. They were willing to offer only a minor league deal, though, which meant that Neshek would have to pitch his way onto the major league 25-man roster to make his $1 million salary.

He knew all about the talented Cardinals pitching staff, but the club offered one advantage over the few teams who had expressed an interest. The Cardinals trained close enough to his home in Melbourne Beach, Florida, that he could commute to work during spring training. The Milwaukee Brewers had made a similar offer, but they trained in Arizona. Neshek wanted to stay close to home because his wife, Stephanee, was pregnant with a due date in late March. The couple had lost their first son, Gehrig, less than 24 hours after he was born on October 2, 2012. The experience was so difficult that it was a year before Stephanee and Pat opened the thousands of cards that fans and friends had sent after Gehrig's death. That the cause of death remained a mystery made staying at home even more of a priority. With the Cardinals 90 minutes south on I-95, Neshek had to rise around 5:00 AM, but he was back home every night. When Stephanee went into labor 11 days before her due date, Neshek was able to drive straight from camp to the hospital and arrived in time for the delivery of Hoyt Robert Neshek (named after the knuckleballer Hoyt Wilhelm), who weighed in at 7 pounds, 11 ounces. The first few days proved to be difficult as Hoyt experienced trouble breathing shortly after birth and had to be assisted by a nasal oxygen mask. He also was diagnosed with pneumonia. "It was real tough," Neshek said. "We didn't hear anything for the first day so we were like, 'What the heck happened?'"

Two days later the air pocket had started to shrink, and the following day, Neshek said Hoyt was "doing very well." Still he had to remain in the hospital for another week to give him the standard 10-day stay for treating pneumonia in newborns. Neshek went back to work on the Monday following the Thursday night birth and continued to pitch like he was a lock to make the team. The reason for his strong spring was clear to Neshek. He rediscovered his fastball.

With the A's Neshek had come to rely on his funky windup and throwing a ton of sliders. After the 2013 season, his dad, Eugene Neshek, suggested he start throwing more fastballs. After dealing with arm injuries, including Tommy John surgery, for the previous four seasons, Neshek had lost faith in his heater, and his strikeout rate dropped to a career-low. "It was really rare if I threw a fastball in a two-week span," Neshek said. "But teams like strikeouts. My dad said, 'You're getting two strikes, you're just not putting guys away. You're not getting the strikeouts like you were when you came up.' We figured we gotta get the fastball back."

Unbeknownst to all those teams seeking bullpen help, Neshek devoted his offseason to finding his fastball. He did not hire a personal trainer or pitching coach to assist him either. He stuck with his usual program of long toss in a park near his home and catch in the backyard with Stephanee, a former collegiate softball player at Mercer, or his dad. When Neshek reported to the Cardinals, pitching coach Derek Lilliquist asked him what happened to that guy who used to hit 94 mph when he came up with the Minnesota Twins in 2006. "Yeah, those were the fun days," Neshek said. "Maybe I can get it back."

By then he had a good idea his heater had returned. He was touching 92 mph in the early days of camp, which, combined with his unorthodox motion, probably seemed more like 100 mph to opposing hitters. Manager Mike Matheny admitted the hopped-up fastball "was something we didn't expect." Neshek not only would make the big league roster, but he also was serving as closer Trevor Rosenthal's primary set-up man before the season was a month old. He walked the only batter he faced on Opening Day and gave up a home run the next day, but then he morphed into a super reliever.

Neshek allowed only one more run until June 3. After giving up one run then, he followed with 18 more scoreless outings. By July 25 he had worked in 46 games and allowed only three runs. He had struck out 42 and walked six in 41⅓ innings, allowing the opposition a paltry .135 batting average and .180 on-base percentage.

The dominance led to another special moment. Neshek was named an All-Star for the first time, and as a bonus the game would be played in his hometown of Minneapolis, where his brother Paul serves on the grounds crew. As Matheny had done in his first two seasons of managing the Cardinals, he held a team meeting to announce the team's All-Star selections. The other three Cardinals—Adam Wainwright, Yadier Molina, and Matt Carpenter—had been named All-Stars before. When Matheny called Neshek's name, the clubhouse erupted in applause. Neshek said he was so stunned that he was lost in the moment. "When he said, 'And going back to his hometown…' that's when everything tuned out," Neshek said. "Wow, it's a reality. It was pretty awesome to see that reaction from the guys."

He would end up as the losing pitcher in Minneapolis after giving up two runs in a third of an inning of work. Neshek also faded a bit down the stretch and he was touched for two costly home runs in the playoffs. In the Cardinals' season-ending 6–3 loss in the National League Championship Series, Neshek served a home run to Mike Morse that turned the Cardinals' 3–2 lead into a 3–3 tie in the eighth inning. Talking to him after that game, Neshek was disappointed but still smiling. "It sucks to be the guy that let them tie it back up," he said. "But I feel great. There's nothing that's going to keep me down."

As we talked inside the visitors' clubhouse at AT&T Park, the long season at its end for the Cardinals, I was reminded of what Neshek had told me early in spring training well before he had made the Cardinals' roster. "I know I'm going to have a good year, and that's a great feeling," he had said. "I feel like I'm intimidating out there. This is going to be a fun year wherever I am."

Lance Lynn Grows Up

On September 6, 2014, Lance Lynn was feeling pretty good about himself as well he should have. Lynn had just pitched six solid innings to defeat the Milwaukee Brewers 5–3 and stay on the best run of his career. His start, though, could not have begun any more poorly. Four pitches in, the Cardinals had made three errors, and the Brewers already had wiped out a 2–0 lead that Matt Adams had provided with a two-run homer in the top of the first.

There had been times when such a defensive breakdown would fluster Lynn, and a two-run inning would escalate into a three- or four-run inning that would send him to an early shower. But Lynn caught a break when Mike Matheny won a replay challenge that turned what would have been a sacrifice fly and a third run into a double play. From then on, Lynn made the right pitch when he needed to and allowed only one more run. That he made it a quality start, even though he was not at his best, said plenty about his growth as a pitcher. "When you don't have your good stuff in a win and you only give up one earned run," he said in the postgame media scrum, "that's a beautiful thing."

The win was Lynn's 15th of the season and earned him the distinction of being the only pitcher to reach that milestone in the National League in each of the past three years. Lynn was not particularly impressed with the feat as he insisted, "The only thing that matters to me is that two of three years thus far we've made the playoffs. That's the only thing that matters." They would, of course, make it three times in three years soon enough.

Lynn is not like so many pitchers who meet the media with the same script of clichés start after start. Ask him a relevant question, and he will offer a meaningful reply. On his best nights, he can fill your audio recorder with an entertaining mixture of dry wit, sarcasm, and insight. This Saturday evening at Miller Park was one of those nights.

Asked what he considered an obvious question about a lack of command after issuing five walks, Lynn replied sarcastically, "No, I just decided to walk them for the hell of it." Not wanting to come off as a jerk, he added, "Yeah, it was command. I was terrible. I was throwing the ball all over the place." When asked if the early adversity was something he might not have been able to overcome earlier in his career, he said with a grin, "I've been great at handling those my whole career. Sometimes you just have bad luck, and that's just terrible when it happens." He even paused for dramatic effect. When asked if he knew the only pitcher in the National League with more wins over the past three years, Lynn did not hesitate. "Our ace," he said, referring to Adam Wainwright. "He's supposed to, isn't he? $19 million a year, I hope so." Asked how he views himself, the man who made a $535,000 salary, said: "Heckuva No. 4 or 5. That's what you guys have been telling me my whole career. For a guy who averages 15 wins, I'm one heckuva 4 or 5."

Lynn did not sound bitter when he brought up Wainwright's contract, but he was not completely joking either. He can read the numbers. For the 48 wins he supplied the Cardinals over three seasons, he was paid a total of $1.53 million. Lynn was not thrilled to have missed out—by days—on being eligible for arbitration in 2013 and the hefty pay raise that would have followed. "They're pretty good at figuring that out to the day," he told me early last summer.

In 2011 he was called up for the first time on June 2, sent down on June 10, and returned for good 12 days later. If not for those 12 days in Memphis, he could have reached Super 2 arbitration status in 2013. Lynn finally cashed in during 2015. The Cardinals bought out his arbitration years by agreeing to a three-year, $22-million deal.

* * *

Pinpointing the day that Michael Lance Lynn took the next step in his career is not difficult. It was May 27, 2014, a Tuesday night at Busch Stadium and he was facing the New York Yankees in his 75th career start.

For the first—and still only—time, Lynn pitched a nine-inning shutout. He allowed only one runner to reach as far as third base while limiting the Yankees to five hits. To that point Lynn had made it through eight innings only twice in his career, and neither time did Matheny let him out for the ninth. Lynn had thrown 116 pitches through eight against the Yankees, but he did not have to work hard to convince his manager to let him go for the complete game. He asked Matheny to give him nine pitches, and the manager said go for it. He knew how badly Lynn wanted to go the distance and sensed a huge confidence boost could be the result. Still, if he had allowed one runner on in the ninth, Lynn would have had been pulled short of the goal. Lynn needed one more pitch than he had asked for, but he still retired the Yankees three up, three down to complete the job. "It's been a big deal for him, something that he's talked a lot about," Matheny said. "We're happy for him."

"Every time you go out, that's what you try to do—not give up any runs and finish it," Lynn said. "Today was the first time I was able to do that. It took me way too long." Lynn received the game ball, heartfelt congratulations from Yadier Molina, and a shaving cream pie to the head during a postgame interview courtesy of Jason Motte. And from Wainwright, who has nine shutouts and 21 complete games on his resume, Lynn received a message. "It's about time," Wainwright told him. Later, Wainwright told me, "You could just tell he was thinking, *If I can get through nine one time, it will be a notch in the belt and a weight removed.* I was that way with my first shutout. I had thrown a couple of complete games but never a shutout. When I finally got one, it was like all right, now we go."

Lynn's season soon took off, too. By staying away from the type of inning that had often cost him, he emerged as the club's most consistent starter. Over his final 21 starts, only once did he allow more than three runs in a game—much less an inning. That was quite a departure from 2012 and 2013 when he was roughed up for three or more runs in one inning 24 times in 62 starts. One difference was pitching, as opposed to merely throwing. Throwing his fastball on 79 percent of his pitches, Lynn still relied on his four-seamer more than any starter in the game except Bartolo Colon. But no longer was Lynn's default mode to simply throw the ball harder when he encountered a rough spot. "If he got into a jam, you knew it, he knew it, people in Africa knew it. He was throwing a four-seam fastball and he was going to throw it at the top of the zone," Wainwright said. "He was going to try to punch you out or pop you up."

Instead of trying to blow away hitters with a 95 mph heater, Lynn began to call on his sinker to induce the ground balls that often result in quick outs in 2014. "When hitters know a pitcher is going to throw it as hard as he can down the middle and they can just wait for him to do that, it makes it easier on them," Lynn says. "If you can sink it, cut it, and make it rise all in one pitch at similar velocities, it's tough. It's going in three different directions."

Lynn also began to better harness his emotions, even if he doesn't like to admit that he sometimes pitched with a hot head when mistakes were made behind him or a hit snuck through a hole or the umpire gypped him of a strike. Although Lynn had not garnered the reputation of, say, the combustible John Lackey, the Cardinals believed there had been times when Lynn would have been better off keeping his gestures to himself. "It wasn't like he wasn't a popular guy on the team, but in the heat of competition, you still want to be respectful to your teammates," general manager John Mozeliak said. "There were times when he seemed frustrated with people." Added Matheny: "You have to be real careful around here. We take a lot of pride in team. We take a lot of pride in how your teammates perceive you."

Lynn, grudgingly, can see where his bosses are coming from. "There's good emotion, and there's bad emotion in this game," he said. "You have to keep the bad from coming out and push it into good emotions that are the right way to do things." He hasn't always been on the same page

Lance Lynn, who went 15–10 with a 2.74 ERA in 2014, throws during Game 2 of the NLCS.

with the Cardinals. In 2012 they thought he carried too much weight on his 6'5" frame, and as a result, he dragged through the dog days. The next season, after he dropped 40 pounds over the offseason, they wondered if he wore down during August. But when he stayed strong throughout the second half in 2014, he admitted he was stronger "physically and mentally" than ever. "That's also part of maturing," Lynn said, "knowing that when you get to those [dog] days, you should work smarter, not harder. Before it was I can do this. So I would do it, and the next thing you know, your next start doesn't feel too hot. That's just part of knowing your body and learning what you need to do to be productive each start."

As for his emotional outbursts, Lynn believes they were a problem mainly because the team did not fully understand him. But when he stifled his emotions, he was not as effective on the mound. Lynn screamed as often as ever in 2014 but at more appropriate times. Instead of looking into his glove and shouting a few expletives if an error were made behind him, Lynn would save such a reaction for an inning-ending strikeout in a key situation. The team has no problem with those showings. "I'm not asking any of these guys to be choirboys," Matheny said.

No one was squawking about Lynn's screaming by the end of 2014. With his newfound consistency resulting in a 2.74 ERA, ninth best in the National League, he quieted all the critics who considered him to be nothing more than a hard-throwing madcap who had benefited from fortuitous run support. "This was a breakthrough year for him," Mozeliak says. "Going back to spring training, he just seemed a little bit different. I mean that in a positive way. He sort of understood everything that was at stake and what he needed to do as a young adult and young professional. Those all met at the right place."

Big City's Roller Coaster

Matt Adams had not been through this in his young career. The Cardinals had lost to the San Francisco Giants 6–4, and a few minutes later, nearly 20 reporters crowded around his locker armed with questions he would rather not answer. Eight days after playing the hero against the Los Angeles Dodgers with a three-run homer, Adams had been the goat against the Giants. On back-to-back plays, the first baseman had made throwing mistakes that resulted in the tying and go-ahead runs for the home team.

Adams had surprised just about everyone with his nimble defense all season and even had Jose Oquendo talking Gold Glove potential. But muffing consecutive throws on fairly routine plays in Game 4 of the National League Championship Series could end such talk for a while.

Trailing 4–3 in the bottom of the sixth, the Giants had put their first two runners on and sacrificed both into scoring position when Gregor Blanco hit an easy grounder to first. Adams backhanded the ball cleanly but made a weak throw home that didn't come close to getting Juan Perez, who had been running on contact. "If I make a good throw, there's a good chance to get an out," Adams said. "I was throwing on the run, off-balance, with a fast runner, but that's no excuse. I threw the ball into the dirt."

With the score now tied and runners on first and third, Joe Panik hit a grounder at Adams down the first-base line. Again, Adams fielded the ball cleanly and stepped on first for out No. 2. But without checking on the runner at third, Adams threw to second in an attempt to turn a double play. The instant the ball left his hand, though, Brandon Crawford bolted from third. Adams' throw went well to the left side of second base, and when Jhonny Peralta caught the ball, he didn't have time to tag Blanco at second or to throw home in an attempt to cut down Crawford. The Giants had the lead. "It's the right play touching the base," Cardinals manager Mike Matheny said. "He's just go to check home at that point.

The runner wasn't going. They took off once he released the ball to second base. That's not the play we want." Adams agreed. "I should have checked Crawford, but it didn't happen," he said.

The day before and just a few lockers away, Adams had watched teammate Randy Choate explain what had gone wrong on his bad throw to first, an error that allowed the Giants to win on a walk-off error. The difference in how Choate and Adams handled the media crunch was as large as the 11-year difference in their experience. Choate spoke clearly and looked his questioner in the eyes. "I threw it where I thought [Kolten Wong] was going to be, and it took off on the left and sailed down the line," Choate said. "Been doing PFPs [pitcher fielding practices] since I was a kid, do them every spring training. It was easy. It was right there, and I blew it." He added: "Anybody in here relishes being in that role. When it works and you're standing here with all these cameras and you won and you did your job, it's awesome. When you're on this side, it sucks."

Unlike Choate, Adams kept the media waiting at his locker for several minutes and then spoke so softly, he was forced to answer the same questions multiple times so everyone could hear. Still, he did not attempt to make an excuse and admitted how costly the plays had been. "Good teams capitalize on mistakes," he said.

Adams bounced back the next night and, as he had done against Clayton Kershaw in the National League Division Series, slugged a home run off a nasty left-hander. This time Adams knocked a curveball from Madison Bumgarner over the right-field fence for only the second homer the Giants ace had served to a lefty all season. The homer had helped the Cardinals take a 3–2 lead in the fourth inning that would hold until the Giants tied it in the eighth and then won in the ninth on a three-run blast by Travis Ishikawa. "I wish we were continuing to play," Adams said afterward. "But it was pretty cool to be part of this club."

Those final days served as a microcosm of sorts for Adams' first season as a regular in the Cardinals' lineup. It was a season of adjustments, of learning to navigate the peaks and valleys of the long season. Adams had to deal with everything from hitting against defensive shifts to producing against left-handed pitchers to fighting through the mental and physical fatigue that occurs during a six-month regular season.

The lefty slugger they call "Big City" handled everything thrown his way, but it wasn't exactly a steady ride. He hit .329 in the first half but stumbled to .235 after the All-Star break, finishing with the second best batting average among Cardinals regulars at .288. He took only nine walks in the first four months before walking 11 times in August. He managed only four home runs in 61 games after the break but blasted three in nine playoff games. He hit .190 against lefties during the regular season but finished as the only left-handed hitter in the majors to homer off Kershaw and Bumgarner.

Through all the highs and lows, the 26-year-old Adams maintained a level-headed approach that belied his lack of experience. "I made some good strides," he said. "There's more to be tapped definitely. Every day I went out there trying to learn some new stuff and trying to get better."

By the second half, Adams had shown the Cardinals enough that they felt secure enough at first base to make a trade they would have been highly unlikely to consider before the season. In need of a veteran starter to fortify their rotation, the Cardinals moved Allen Craig to the Boston Red Sox in a deal that brought them John Lackey. Though Craig was having an off year, he had been one of the National League's top run producers over the previous two seasons with a .427 batting average with runners in scoring position was far and away the best in the majors. Adams' efforts did not make Craig expendable, but they made moving him tolerable. "If Matt was having a horrible year, maybe that trade wouldn't have been so smart because it's not like we have a true first baseman in the works," general manager John Mozeliak said. "As well as Matt's played, we were pretty excited that he could handle this."

The No. 1 reason the Cardinals believe that Adams can become a fixture at first base is his picturesque swing that is equal parts short, smooth, and sweet. "It's perfect," Cardinals hitting coach John Mabry said. "If you want to build one, build that one. It's real easy, it's real repeatable. It's fluid, it's powerful. It's everything you want as a swing."

Manager Mike Matheny was a special assistant in player development with the Cardinals when he first saw Adams in the summer of 2011 and quickly was impressed. "I remember watching the ball jump off his bat," Matheny said. "I remember saying this kid reminds me of Jim Thome and I still say the same thing. He has that smooth, effortless swing, and the ball jumps off the bat with backspin and carry."

Adams hit .300 with 32 homers and 101 RBIs for Double A Springfield that season, a feat made more remarkable by the fact that he skipped a level of Single A. "We don't typically do that, especially with offensive players, because the test of the Florida State League is always such a good one," Mozeliak said. "Yet he had had such a prolific year and strong spring, everybody felt comfortable giving him a chance. Obviously, it was a very smart decision."

Adams' swing barely has altered since he was a 10-year-old slugging homers against the older kids in Philipsburg, Pennsylvania. His offseason hitting coach, Justin Hazelton, checked footage of Adams hitting when he was a sophomore in high school and then as a sophomore at Slippery Rock University. Hoping to see how the swing had evolved, they were pleasantly disappointed. "It's almost exactly the same," Adams said.

The road from a Division II school to the big leagues has gone as smoothly as Adams could have hoped. Well, lasting until the 23rd round of the 2009 draft wasn't part of the plan, but that was out of his control. Adams could not stop teams from thinking his .495 batting average and 1.419 on-base plus slugging percentage (OPS) as a junior were overly inflated because he played at a small school. Neither could he convince teams that his stoutness would not be a hindrance.

But Adams had a fan in Cardinals scout Brian Hopkins, who had seen him several times his junior year and believed his hitting would play in the pros. The Cardinals were prepared to take him sooner, but based on what they were hearing from other clubs, they weren't overly concerned he would continue to fall. They grabbed him two rounds after they drafted Trevor Rosenthal, who is now their closer.

A week later Adams had a $25,000 signing bonus and was on the way to Johnson City, Tennessee. Though catcher had been his primary position in college, he learned that he had changed positions upon arriving in Tennessee. He was now a first baseman. Adams hit .365 in his first month and was promoted to Batavia, where he hit .346. At both stops he also showed enough power that already he was easing any doubts about his small school background. "You could tell right away that his swing was different," said Nick Greenwood, a Cardinals reliever who spent parts of three seasons in the minors with Adams. "I knew he was a big leaguer as soon as I saw him. There was just a different sound when the ball came off his bat. You can see it here, too. When he gets into one, you know it's gone."

History revisionists might look at the offseason following 2011 and say that Adams' presence allowed the Cardinals to look differently at the Albert Pujols free-agent negotiations. But they would be wrong. The Cardinals wanted Pujols to stay in St. Louis and were disappointed when he left. Although Adams certainly took note of the hole left by Pujols' departure, he did not feel like all roadblocks had been removed from his way to the majors. "There was still Craiger," Adams said. And Craig assumed first base as soon as the Cardinals signed Carlos Beltran shortly after Pujols left for the Angels. "I felt like if they want me up here, they're going to find a spot for me," Adams said. "But if that wasn't my time, then I still had to work hard in the minor leagues and try to improve."

Because of an injury to Lance Berkman, Adams was called up for the first time in May of 2012 and spent a month in the big leagues. He returned for good when he made the Cardinals out of spring training in 2013 and responded by hitting .284 with 17 homers in spot duty. Before long Berkman figured the rookie was due a nickname. Instead of opting for the rather obvious "Big Country" that combined Adams' physique with his upbringing, Berkman went in a different direction. "He was tired of Big Country," Adams said. "So he put a different spin on it with Big City. I showed up one day, and he started calling me that. David Freese fell in love with it and kept the ball rolling."

The Taveras Tragedy

When Oscar Taveras wasn't in the batter's box, he always seemed to be smiling. His was a slightly goofy grin, reminiscent of a kid who was living his dream. Taveras was five years old when he told his dad that he would play in the major leagues, and here he was at the age of 22, hitting a home run in the 2014 National League Championship Series.

Two weeks after the young slugger had thrilled Busch Stadium with a pinch-hit homer in the NLCS, he was killed in a single-car crash near his home in the Dominican Republic. According to authorities Taveras was driving his 2014 Chevrolet Camaro at an excessive speed on a rain-slicked highway and slammed into a tree. He was taken to Cabarete Medical Center and pronounced dead. His 18-year-old girl-friend, identified as Edilia Arvelo, was with him and also died in the wreck. Toxicology reports showed that Taveras was illegally intoxicated with a blood-alcohol level five times greater than the .05 legal limit in the Dominican Republic. Taveras and Arvelo were returning from a Sunday afternoon cookout at a nearby river, according to reports.

Thousands attended Taveras' funeral two days after his death in his hometown of Sousa, a small beachside community on the northern side of the Dominican Republic. The Cardinals were represented by general manager John Mozeliak, manager Mike Matheny, and international scouting director Moises Rodriguez. Taveras' closest friend on the team, fellow Dominican Carlos Martinez, also attended the service. Martinez told American reporters that day that Taveras had a penchant for driving—and living—too fast. The day before the fatal wreck, Martinez said he had invited Taveras to spend time with him at a beachside resort. Taveras refused, choosing instead to spend Sunday afternoon with friends from his hometown. "I'd tell him about being in the big leagues and acting like a professional all of the time, but it didn't stick," Martinez told mlb.com. "He would listen to the advice, but he just wouldn't put it into practice."

The Cardinals had endured sudden, tragic deaths of active players twice in recent years. Starting pitcher and team leader Darryl Kile, who had 90 percent blockage in two of his coronary arteries, died in his sleep in a hotel room when the Cardinals were on a trip in Chicago in 2002, and reliever Josh Hancock was killed in a car wreck hours after a game at Busch Stadium in 2007. Hancock was a couple of miles from the ballpark driving west on I-64 when he slammed a rented SUV into a tow truck that had stopped in the left lane to assist a motorist. The 29-year-old, who authorities said died almost instantly, had a blood-alcohol level reported at .157 that was well over the .08 allowable limit. Soon after his death, the Cardinals banned alcohol from their clubhouse.

That alcohol factored into Taveras' death did not lessen the heartbreak of those who knew him, Mozeliak said. "This was a tragedy and one that you would like to think could have been prevented," Mozeliak said. "But accidents do happen, and what was involved in it is disappointing, but in the end, it's still a tragedy."

Because Taveras was home and on his own time, the Cardinals could have done little to prevent the accident, but Mozeliak hoped the organization's players would take away a lesson.

"After the Hancock situation, we tried to be aggressive on this front, and that hasn't changed," Mozeliak said. "We try to emphasize making smart decisions not only on the field but off the field. Will this re-energize us to make sure that we stress that? Absolutely. What I hope comes out of this is these young players—that have the pedigree of being considered great—realize that they're not bulletproof. That they understand that they have to be careful and that they understand that they need to be smart about their everyday decisions."

Taveras was scheduled to be home for only another week before reporting to the Cardinals' spring training base in Jupiter, Florida, to begin offseason conditioning. Before he headed home, Mozeliak and Matheny had met with the young slugger to talk about their expectations and what he needed to work on. Taveras had been considered one of the game's top hitting prospects for the past three years but had hit a somewhat disappointing .239 in his rookie season. Still, the club's expectations remained great. "He can be a star," Matheny said shortly after the season.

Taveras had not played in the major leagues for long, but his death deeply affected the baseball world. Within hours after news reached St. Louis, fans started a memorial at the base of the Stan Musial statue outside the third-base gate at Busch Stadium. On the night he was buried, in an otherwise dark Busch Stadium, the Cardinals kept on a bank of lights in right field where Taveras had been stationed weeks earlier. That same night before Game 6 at the World Series, a moment of silence was held, and the starting pitcher for the Kansas City Royals, Yordano Ventura, had written on his cap, "RIP O.T. #18."

Ventura pitched seven shutout innings with the Royals facing elimination and afterward dedicated his victory to Taveras, whom he considered a close friend. They had met when both were playing in the minor leagues, and in 2012 the two became close enough that Ventura stayed in Taveras' apartment whenever his team played the Cardinals' affiliate in Springfield, Missouri. Less than a week after Taveras debuted in the majors in 2014, the Cardinals played an interleague series in Kansas City, and Ventura's mom prepared Taveras a Dominican meal.

Inside the World Series interview room at Kansas City's Kauffman Stadium, Ventura draped a Dominican Republic flag over the front of the table before he began his postgame news conference. "I carry my emotions on my sleeve and I did it for the whole country of the Dominican Republic," Ventura said. "I'm proud to be a Dominican…If he was still here, I for sure would be talking to him. Oscar would be very happy for me and very proud. Oscar was a very humble guy and very likeable, and I'm going to miss him a lot. I'm grieving and I want to send my best thoughts to his family. This is hard for me."

Matheny took the loss of Taveras so hard that when the club asked him the night of the crash to say something that could be included in a press release, he declined. "I simply couldn't," he said the next day when he issued a poignant passage via the Cardinals. "First of all, it felt like a bad dream that could not be real, and when reality kicked in, my words didn't even seem to make sense," Matheny wrote. "To say this is a horrible loss of a life ended too soon would be an understatement. To talk about the potential of his abilities seemed to be untimely. All I wanted to do was get the guys together and be with our baseball family. I know the hurt that comes along with buying into the brotherhood of a baseball team. That hurt is just as powerful as the joys that come with this life. Not to say it is even close to the depth of pain his true family is going through, but the pain itself is just as real. The ache is deep because the relationships were deep and forged through time and trials. In my opinion the word 'love' is the most misused and misunderstood word in the English language. It is not popular for men to use this word and even less popular for athletes. But there is not a more accurate word for how a group of men share a deep and genuine concern for each other. We loved Oscar, and he loved us. That is what a team does, that is what a family does. You will be missed, Oscar."

Taveras' death changed the Cardinals' plans for the offseason and led to a touching switching of uniform numbers. The player for whom they traded to take over right field, Jason Heyward, wore the same number—No. 22—as Matheny. Matheny gave up the number and took No. 44, which had been used by Martinez in 2014. To acquire Heyward, the Cardinals traded starting pitcher Shelby Miller to the Atlanta Braves. The trade of Miller would open a spot in the rotation for Martinez, who was switching to No. 18, the number that had been worn by his good friend.

PART II:
2013

Cardinals Record: 97–65

*Cardinals Finish: Won NLCS against
Los Angeles Dodgers*

Won NLDS against Pittsburgh Pirates

Carpenter Becomes a Leadoff Hitter

On May 2, 2013, the Cardinals scored six runs in the third inning on the way to a 6–5 victory at Milwaukee that would be remembered as the night good-guy right-hander Jake Westbrook won his 100th game. But for the Cardinals, the day would become much more notable for more than Westbrook's milestone win. That was the day Matt Carpenter was moved to the top of the batting order once and for all, a move that would change his career and transform the Cardinals offense.

Mike Matheny had tried Carpenter in the leadoff spot during the season's first month but was not ready to give up on Jon Jay. But when Jay went 0-for-4 and his average dropped to .204 the previous day, Matheny again opted for Carpenter. He responded by singling in his first two at-bats and scoring in the game-breaking third inning, and Matheny hasn't seen a reason to try anyone else in the top spot since.

Carpenter has become arguably the game's most productive leadoff hitter. Over the rest of 2013 and all of 2014, he ranked first among all leadoff men in runs, hits, walks, and doubles. He also saw more pitches than any leadoff hitter and reached base more than any hitter in the National League. With that kind of production, the Cardinals could care less that Carpenter has stolen a total of eight bases, a total that might have been a good weekend back in the days of Vince Coleman. "They just told me to be myself," Carpenter said late in 2013. "That's really what I've done. I've continued to stick with what's been working."

That Carpenter made such a successful transition in the batting order should not be a surprise. He had shown his adaptability in the field when he moved from third base to second base and made the All-Star team in what was his first season as an everyday player. When he went back to third in 2014, he made the All-Star team again. "I just want to be known as a ballplayer," he said.

It's been that way since he was old enough to walk. He grew up in a baseball family with his father, Rick, a highly successful high school

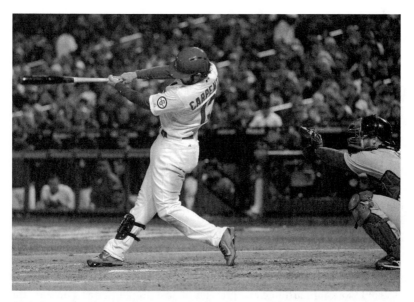

Matt Carpenter, who made his first All-Star team in 2013 while recording a .318 batting average and 55 doubles, hits an RBI single against the Boston Red Sox during Game 4 of the 2013 World Series.

coach. His mom, Tammie, a former high school softball player, toted Matt and his siblings to as many games as she could manage. Tammie could tell that Matt was different at a very young age. "When he was two or three, he would sit on my lap behind home plate and make comments like 'Mom, that guy needs to move over a little bit or he needs to do this,'" Tammie Carpenter said. "It was weird, but he just had an eye for that. He knew what was going on. My other son, Tyler, who also was drafted, probably had the most ability, but he didn't have the same mental outlook. When we would be at games, he would be over there playing in the dirt with cars while Matt would be sitting in my lap watching every move. I knew he had this special thing about him."

Carpenter grew up and played for his dad at Lawrence Elkins High

School near Houston, where they won two state championships, and Rick was named *USA TODAY*'s 2002 National Coach of the Year. Matt was not drafted out of high school but was the top recruit at Texas Christian University, where he would spend five years. The first two and a half were not his best. Carpenter did not apply himself in class, did not take care of himself, and generally was falling short of coach Jim Schlossnagle's expectations on as well as off the field. Early in his junior season, Matt tore a ligament in his right elbow and underwent Tommy John surgery. He had arrived at a crossroads.

Schlossnagle had met with Carpenter numerous times to convince him to apply himself more in school and baseball, but little changed. But after the injury, with Carpenter's parents on hand, Matt finally took to heart what his coach had to say. Overnight, he changed his diet and started working hard in class. He says he lost 40 pounds and became the first guy to arrive at practice and the last to leave and also would earn his degree in communications.

Carpenter, however, didn't wow the scouts in his comeback year and ended up spending a fifth year at TCU. After a solid senior season, he lasted until the 13th round before the Cardinals drafted him and offered a $1,000 signing bonus. The Cardinals could make such a trivial offer because Carpenter had no bargaining power. Finished with college he could sign with the Cardinals or find a real job.

He took the bonus, reported to rookie ball, and made a steady climb through the system. He reached the majors in 2011 and arrived to stay in 2012. He moved to second base in 2013 and enjoyed a breakout season, finishing fourth in National League MVP voting while leading the majors in runs scored and doubles and tying for the lead in hits.

Carpenter came up short in the last weekend of the regular season, though, when he went 0 for his final 8 and finished one hit short of 200. He admitted that he had put pressure on himself to hit the milestone, but more than that, he had just worn down. Not only had he played in

157 games, but he also had continued to spend more time at the ballpark than anyone except for possibly his manager.

Toward the end of the 2014 season, Carpenter said he had learned to better pace himself and he showed he had plenty left for the postseason. He hit four homers in nine playoff games after hitting eight all season. As he had in Game 6 of the 2013 National Championship Series, Carpenter also had a game-turning, epic at-bat against Dodgers ace Clayton Kershaw that ended in a three-run double that completed the Cardinals' remarkable comeback from a 6–1 deficit.

How much Carpenter actually reduced his pre and postgame work, however, was a matter of opinion. When Matheny wanted to be sure Carpenter had some down time, he had to order him. "He's still out of control," Matheny said. "That's just who he is. 'Of thine own self be true.' That's how he got here."

The payoff came early in spring training of 2014, when Carpenter officially became part of the Cardinals' core by agreeing to a six-year, $52 million extension that keeps him under contract through 2019. His deal followed the extensions signed by Adam Wainwright in 2013 and Yadier Molina in 2012. Both of those players, along with Matt Holliday, attended the press conference at Roger Dean Stadium as a show of support. And, perhaps, to zing him a bit.

At one point in the presser, Holliday raised his hand to ask a question. He wanted to know if Carpenter now would now have the resources for a second car during spring training so his wife, Mackenzie, would not have to shuttle him to the ballpark at 5:00 every morning. "There's been a lot of sacrifices involved," Carpenter answered after the room had quieted. "But we might look into that."

Another reason that Carpenter is a rare player is his refusal to wear batting gloves. He never has—not even at TCU where aluminum bats could make hitting in cold weather quite unpleasant. In a game at Colorado Springs, on a day when the temperature was freezing and the wind was howling, he tried to wear them. "He put them on for an at-bat, and that was it," Schlossnagle said.

Carpenter remains close to his TCU roots, literally as well as figuratively. He and his wife, Mackenzie, bought a home across the street from the center-field wall at Lupton Stadium. Carpenter often is the first to arrive in the team's weight room during the offseason. "He's a self-made player," Schlossnagle said. "That doesn't mean he's not talented, but he's a self-made player, and I don't think that will ever change. He's the perfect combination of confident and humble." Said Matheny: "That's just who he is. His work is out of control in the weight room, out on the field, in the cage."

Carpenter has no trouble making whatever adjustments are needed to stay at the level he's reached. The more he has hit out of the leadoff spot, the more disciplined he has become at the plate. He understands a key part of the role is to take enough pitches in order for the hitters behind him to gain a feel for the pitcher's stuff. No accident that Carpenter swung at the first pitch less than any hitter in the National League in 2014, just 8 percent of the time.

He showed that same patience at TCU, and it wasn't always encouraged. Hitting in the middle of the order, Carpenter took more pitches than his coach wanted. "It's funny. All of the things that he's really good at as a major league player are the things that I used to yell at him for as a college player," Schlossnagle said. "I needed him to hit. He would get in 3–1 counts with a runner on first and second, and the next pitch would be right there and most left-handed hitters are swinging. But he takes it, and now we have the bases loaded for the next guy. More than once, I told him, 'The next guy is not as good as you. I need you to swing.'"

His plate discipline backfired on Carpenter at times in 2014, too. Because he rarely offered at borderline pitches, even with two strikes, his strikeouts went up as well as his walks. Carpenter, though, believes in his approach. "If you can't hit it hard, what's the point?" He said. "If a guy makes a pitch that's a borderline strike that if I swing at, odds are I'm going to put it in play softly. But if it's borderline, there's a 50-50 chance it will be called a ball, and you're on first base. Situations where I took a pitch that I think should have been called a ball, and it was called a strike, it is what it is. You can't harp on it. You move on. I'm going to continue with my same approach."

Shelby Nears Perfection

On his fifth pitch of the eighth start of his career, Shelby Miller threw a 94 mph fastball on the inner half of the plate that was right where he intended. The pitch broke the bat of Colorado Rockies leadoff hitter Eric Young, but somehow the ball still dropped into shallow right field for a single. And that was all the offense the Colorado Rockies managed on the night of May 10, 2013. Miller faced 27 more batters, and all 27 made outs. In his second month as a full-time starter, the young right-hander had pitched one of the best games ever by a St. Louis Cardinal.

Since right-hander George Bradley no-hit the Hartford Dark Blues on July 15, 1876, in what is considered the first no-hitter in major league history, there had been 10 no-nos thrown by Cardinals pitchers. Of those, Paul Dean in 1934 pitched the only one that matched Miller's gem in allowing a lone base runner. In 1989 right-hander Jose DeLeon pitched 11 innings against the Reds and allowed only one hit without a walk, but the Cardinals lost 2–0 in 13 innings. Lefty Steve Carlton threw a one-hit, no-walk shutout against the Cubs in 1968, but he also hit a batter, doubling the number of base runners allowed by Miller.

Ranking how Miller's masterpiece fits in Cardinals history is debatable. Determining the key to his success is not. Miller built his near perfecto around his fastball. Of the 113 pitches he threw, 92 were tracked as fastballs, according to the pitch-by-pitch on mlb.com. The "slowest" was timed at 92 mph, the fastest at 97. His final pitch, a called strike three to Young, registered at 95 mph. Miller finished all 13 of his strikeouts with fastballs, eight of them with the Rockies looking. In the first and the fourth innings, the Rockies' top hitters—Carlos Gonzalez and Troy Tulowitzki—both took strike three fastballs. "Barely strikes," said Gonzalez, who wasn't griping about the umpire, "it wasn't like he was leaving the pitch right down the middle. He was hitting corners. It was impressive."

As impressive as it was, the outing might also have stalled Miller's progress as a big league starter. After dominating the National League's leading offense with his fastball, Miller understandably became a little smitten with his heater. His secondary pitches weren't completely neglected, but they were underused, which resulted in a couple of issues. One, hitters began to sit on his fastball, and two, not throwing his secondary pitches very often slowed their development. Miller finished his rookie season with 15 wins and a 3.06 ERA, but no question his effectiveness slipped as the season wore on.

In 104⅔ innings in the first half of his rookie season, Miller averaged 9.6 strikeouts and 2.5 walks per nine innings while allowing 10 homers. In the second half, he served the same number of homers in far fewer innings—68⅔—and his strikeout rate dropped to 7.5 while his walk rate rose to 3.7.

Miller became the forgotten man in October, appearing only once as a reliever in the Cardinals' postseason run to the World Series. While the media speculated he was shut down because of an innings limit and Mike Matheny said Miller came close several times to getting in a game, there's little doubt the Cardinals would have found work for him if he had finished the regular season stronger.

Miller's disappearance in October created the potential for an awkward situation in November. Miller was being married shortly after the season and had invited Matheny to the ceremony. The manager was happy to oblige, even though he knew he would be amongst a large gathering of Miller fans that might want an explanation about his non-use in the postseason. Matheny took the initiative, however, and offered an explanation to several in the groom's family, even though they didn't ask. Matheny also stepped in and handled the invocation before dinner, leaving everyone in attendance with little reason to question his motives.

For much of 2014, Miller struggled to find the form he'd shown in the first half of his rookie season. He went into spring training preparing to work deeper into games, but he didn't have great success. Miller made it through six innings in only about 40 percent of his starts through July and was even moved to the bullpen for a brief stretch around the All-Star break.

At the urging of his coaches and teammates, Miller had started to mix in a sinker with his fastball but wasn't getting the results that he wanted or the club needed. But when the club traded for Justin Masterson, a noted sinkerball specialist, he passed on a grip that felt comfortable to Miller. While Masterson's pitching was a bust in his short stay in St. Louis, his influence on Miller could have a lasting impact.

Armed with a new and improved sinker, Miller did his best pitching in the final six weeks of 2014. He pitched so well that when the Cardinals went shopping for a right fielder, the Atlanta Braves made sure they acquired Miller in return for slugger Jason Heyward. Over Miller's final six regular season starts with the Cardinals, he averaged better than six innings an outing, posted a 1.69 ERA, and worked seven scoreless innings in back-to-back starts for the first time. He was quick to credit the sinker. "It's been the difference-maker," Miller said. "I feel like I'm pitching a lot more."

By that, Miller meant pitching as opposed to merely throwing. But before he was dealt, he would be pitching a little more for the Cardinals— in October. Miller never complained about his lack of use in the 2013 postseason, admitting only that he wasn't sure what was going on. But he was counting on being used this time around. He was hanging out in the clubhouse lunchroom before the Cardinals flew to Los Angeles for the start of the National League Division Series when Matheny gave him the word. "It was not a big deal at all," Miller said. "He just came up to me and said you've got Game 4."

It, though, would be a big deal. The first start of his playoff career would come against Dodgers ace Clayton Kershaw with a chance to send the Cardinals to the National League Championship Series. Miller matched Kershaw with five scoreless innings before running into trouble in the sixth. He would end up allowing five hits and three walks in five and two-third innings, putting the Cardinals in a 2–0 hole that they would overcome in dramatic fashion in the seventh. "It was pretty special," Miller said during the Cardinals' clubhouse celebration. "Everything I thought it would be."

Or, as his manager called it, an "I told you so" moment. "Going out and pitching like he did, he was telling us that he could have done it last year. We just didn't give him the opportunity," Matheny said.

Historic in the Clutch

By Memorial Day in 2013, a day seldom passed when Mike Matheny or one of his players was not asked about their hitting in the clutch. There was good reason for the line of questioning. As a team, the Cardinals entered June hitting an extraordinary .342 with runners in scoring position (RISP). Overall, the Cardinals were hitting a very respectable .274. But when they put a runner on second and/or third, their batting average improved by 68 points. It was unbelievable, historic, and—apparently—inexplicable. "I don't know. It's nothing that I try to explain," said Allen Craig, the leader of the Cardinals' clutch club. "I have my approach. I have my routine. I just go about my business and let it happen."

It happened for the entire season. The Cardinals finished 2013 hitting .330 with RISP—by far the best mark since the major statistic providers began tracking the split in 1974. Only the 2007 Detroit Tigers and the 1996 Colorado Rockies, both who finished at .311, have come within 20 points of the Cardinals' record. St. Louis' hitting with two outs and runners in scoring position was just as remarkable with a .305 average that was 47 points better than the next-best team in 2013.

In just their sixth game, the Cardinals gave their first indication that this could be a unique season in the RISP department. On a Sunday afternoon when the San Francisco Giants received their World Series rings at AT&T Park, the Cardinals pounded the champions 14–3 to clinch the opening weekend series and gain a little revenge for losing the 2012 National League Championship Series. The Cardinals did not homer, which would become another recurring theme in their season, but they cranked out 10 hits in 14 at-bats with runners in scoring position. They knocked out Giants ace Matt Cain with a nine-run fourth inning that included six hits, a walk, a hit by pitch, and a sacrifice fly that all came with runners in scoring position. "We just keep fighting and fighting and we take what they give you and try not to do too much," said manager Mike Matheny during his postgame presser. "If there was a wish for what kind of offense we have, that'd be it."

That wish would come true. Nineteen times in 2013 the Cardinals scored at least 10 runs. They would do so three times in 2014, a feat made more impressive considering they hit the fourth fewest homers in the major leagues. In 49 games they collected at least four hits with RISP compared to 25 in 2014. They lost only three of them. No surprise, the 2013 Cardinals also led the league in runs scored for what would be the second time in three seasons.

Craig finished the season hitting .454 with RISP, a mark bettered by only George Brett and Tony Gwynn since 1974. But the cleanup man had plenty of help. Of the major leagues' 10 leading hitters with runners in scoring position in 2013, five wore the Birds on the Bat. In addition to Craig were Matt Holliday, Matt Carpenter, Carlos Beltran, and Yadier

Molina, all with RISP averages between .373 and .390. Remarkably, only one regular—David Freese—finished the season with a lower RISP average than overall average: .238 to .262. Even light-hitting shortstop Pete Kozma delivered in the clutch with a .322 RISP average compared to .217 overall.

Opponents that visited Busch Stadium during the second half would be queried for an explanation almost as much as the home team. When the Los Angeles Dodgers came to St. Louis in July, Clayton Kershaw admitted, "It's kind of miraculous that they've done that for this long in the season." But asked how they could, Kershaw shrugged. "It means they have good hitters," he said.

Hitting guru Charlie Manuel, then manager of the Philadelphia Phillies, credited the Cardinals' willingness to hit the ball to the opposite field for their run-producing prowess. San Diego Padres manager Bud Black pointed to the low strikeout totals of Cardinals hitters, who finished with the second fewest strikeouts in the National League. The Padres also noticed that St. Louis hitters became more aggressive at the plate in run-scoring opportunities. "They want to score quick," starting pitcher Eric Stults said. "We talked about it before, trying to eliminate a big inning and slowing things down when they get guys on base. They get up there and they want to swing early. They want to score early."

Though each of the theories made some sense, the Cardinals did not agree. They insisted their approach remained basically the same regardless of how many men were on base. To Matheny and hitting coach John Mabry, it was all about the process. "We focus on preparing mentally every single pitch," Matheny said. "Guys are given a good, clear message from Mabes on what they're trying to do. They talk through it, they walk through it, and they practice it relentlessly. Then they have the freedom when they walk in the box. They're prepared and hopefully they execute a good plan. They know what they're trying to do. Now go up there and have a relentless at-bat."

The suggestion that the Cardinals concentrated more when the stakes were higher was considered insulting to the club because it implied they didn't consider their other at-bats as important. "Some strange way that could look negatively on me, which I don't get," Craig said. "I feel like I have the same focus every time. I've just had a lot of opportunities with runners on base this year."

Craig, though, had fewer opportunities than a lot of hitters. Sixty-two players finished 2013 with more at-bats with runners in scoring position than Craig's 130 but only one, Miguel Cabrera, had more hits (62 to 59). The season at the time was not regarded as a fluke for Craig either. He had led the majors in 2012 by hitting .400 with RISP. He was asked so many times about his success that he eventually came up with a theory, though it didn't sound much different than his strategy of hitting with the bases empty. "The name of the game is giving yourself the best chance to succeed," he said. "If you're trying to pull the ball in that [RISP] situation, you leave yourself susceptible to anything away. It's always good to keep the ball in the middle of the field. That's not to say I never try to pull the ball with runners in scoring position, but for the most part, it's trying to hit the ball hard on a line somewhere."

The one aspect of the team's RISP success that most agreed on was that repeating the performance would be highly unlikely. General manager John Mozeliak called it an outlier and said, "Enjoy the ride as we take it." Only Matheny continued to insist that a repeat would be possible. Of course, if he had admitted the RISP success was a statistical anomaly, he would be sending his players the wrong message. He would in effect be telling them that he did not believe they could sustain it.

They didn't sustain it, though, the following year. In 2014 the Cardinals hit a middle-of-the-pack .254 with runners in scoring position, just one point above their overall batting average.

El Hombre Visits

As it turns out, you can take Albert Pujols off the Cardinals, but you can't get him to leave St. Louis. Lured by a $254 million contract, Pujols left for the Los Angeles Angels after the 2011 season, but he and his family have kept a home in a St. Louis County suburb. Pujols has maintained a presence with his foundation in St. Louis, too. One event that lives on, though with a new name, is the annual golf tournament that benefits the Pujols Family Foundation. His day job kept him from attending the tournament in 2014, but Pujols made it home for the event in his first two years with the Angels.

The tournament now is hosted by and carries the name of Matt Holliday, who also has limited days off at home during the baseball season. But thanks to the schedule-makers, the Cardinals and the Angels both were idle on a steamy Monday morning the week before the All-Star break. Even though the Angels had played on Sunday night at home, Pujols and several of his teammates, including Mike Trout, arrived at the Meadowbrook Country Club around 9:00 AM the next morning.

The Cardinals were well represented at the event, too, as you would expect. Among those golfing was Adam Wainwright, who just four days earlier had pitched against Pujols for the first time. The outing had not ended well for Wainwright, thanks to his former teammate. Still, after making his way to the practice range, Wainwright idled up to Pujols and gave him a hug befitting former teammates who remain friends. Wainwright then stepped back and, a bit sheepishly, began to talk about pitching against Pujols during that series.

Three times Wainwright had retired Pujols on grounders to the left side of the infield. But in the ninth, with the Cardinals leading 5–3, Pujols came through with a hit off Wainwright that started a winning rally for the Angels. As soon as Wainwright mentioned the ninth inning, Pujols could not resist. He jabbed Wainwright for his pitch selection. With a wide smile, he told Wainwright that he had thrown him one

Once beloved by the Cardinal faithful, Albert Pujols takes a swing during his first series against St. Louis as a member of the Los Angeles Angels.

curveball too many. Wainwright had gotten Pujols to roll over a curve in the sixth inning and used two more to get ahead of him 1–2 leading off the bottom of the ninth. Pujols then laid off a cutter to even the count at 2–2. On the next pitch, the sixth of the at-bat, Wainwright stayed with a cutter-curve pattern and fed Pujols a curve that he lined—softly—to left to give the Angels hope for a rally. Though the single was his first and only hit of the three-game series, Pujols had guessed correctly. "Why didn't you blow that cutter or a fastball by me," Pujols asked. "That's what you should have done. Another curve? I got that."

Wainwright had no answer.

After Pujols' single Mike Matheny then turned the game over to Edward Mujica, who entered having gone 21-for-21 in save chances after moving into the closer's role early in the season. Mujica promptly served a two-run homer to Josh Hamilton that tied the game, and five batters later, Erick Aybar's single gave the Angels a walk-off victory.

Pujols and his contingent would not have long to gloat in St. Louis. The Angels would be playing at Wrigley Field on Tuesday, which left Pujols just enough time to stop by his home and make an appearance on behalf of his foundation. "It's always good to be back," he said. "Just because we went out to Southern California, this is home for us."

Resentment still lingered in St. Louis over Pujols' departure but at least one in attendance at the golf event, Matheny, used the occasion to voice his support of the former Cardinals icon. The Cardinals manager said that he wished that Pujols' detractors would start to look past the business part of the game and remember what the slugger had done and was still doing for the area. "I do believe time will heal all this," Matheny said. "People will realize these are good people. The business side of baseball clouds things up sometimes for everybody, but you can't get away from the fact that these people are investing their time, their resources, and their platform to making a difference in our community."

Big Mac Returns

The buzz in the press box started to spread before batting practice: Mark McGwire said he would talk. For a sports writer, the possibility of interviewing McGwire was more exciting than a free buffet—especially under the circumstances on this day in August of 2013. This was Big Mac's first time back in Busch Stadium since he had taken the job as hitting coach for the Los Angeles Dodgers. Because he had accepted the job during the previous offseason, McGwire had not addressed the St. Louis media since his departure.

But that wasn't the main reason the media was looking to talk with him. In a whopper of a coincidence, McGwire had returned to his old stomping grounds on the very day that Major League Baseball had handed out punishment for the most wide-ranging performance-enhancing drug scandal yet. Thirteen suspensions totaling 811 games had been announced as a result of MLB's investigation into the Biogenesis anti-aging clinic. Among the implicated were some of the game's biggest names, including Alex Rodriguez and Ryan Braun.

Whatever McGwire would have to say would be newsworthy not only in St. Louis, but also across the baseball landscape. He had been one of the faces of the steroid era when he was playing for the Cardinals, a record-setting slugger who later disgraced himself at a congressional hearing for not wanting to talk about the past. Then, nearly five years later as he was preparing for a return to the game, McGwire went on television and admitted what most already assumed. Yes, he had taken PEDs for years during his playing career.

Moments after the Dodgers finished their batting practice, McGwire did not disappoint the two dozen media types that had converged in the visitors' dugout. He plopped down, leaned his back against the wall, and said in so many words—bring it on.

First question: "What is your reaction to the suspensions that were handed out today?"

He smiled…a little. "I was really hoping the first question would be how does it feel to come back to St. Louis," he said.

Sensing that wasn't going to be asked, he answered, anyway. "Well, it feels great to be here in St. Louis."

Then the big man turned serious and for the next 15 minutes, he answered every question. He was thoughtful, he was emotional at times, and he was candid, far more so than that day on Capitol Hill in March of 2005, when he so famously said, "I'm not here to talk about the past."

Interviewing McGwire felt like asking someone to dredge up a part of their life they'd wish had not happened, but so what? That was part of the price to pay. Steroids put such a black mark on the game for so long that anyone who benefited from them should be put under the spotlight. But give McGwire credit because his regret seemed sincere. "I really hope and pray that this is the end of it," he said. "Everybody, especially the players, they really don't want any part of it. They all hope this is the end of it."

The most poignant question was asked by the late Bryan Burwell, a columnist for the *St. Louis Post-Dispatch* who for years had criticized baseball for the steroids era. Burwell asked if he felt like he helped start this whole PED mess? "That's a tough question," McGwire said after a long pause. "Wish I was never part of it." He also said using PEDs was not worth it "at all."

McGwire had practically been driven into hiding after his unfortunate testimony before a congressional panel. His public appearances were few and far between. Plus, McGwire long ago realized that despite ranking 10th on the all-time list of home run leaders, his chances of making the Hall of Fame have been reduced to about nil because of steroids. His name has appeared on the Hall of Fame ballot nine times, and he has yet to receive more than 23.6 percent of the votes, far short of the 75 percent needed for induction. "Unfortunately, I don't believe there will be a day that I'll be in there," he said. "That's okay. It's the way things are. I've dealt with it. I'm okay with it."

Did he think players today have less tolerance for PED users than when he played? "Yes, absolutely," he said. "That's good, really good. [Evan] Longoria said today it's one of the saddest days in baseball. It is. It's really bad."

Clearly, the interview session was uncomfortable for McGwire, who had the strained look of someone who was on trial. He was known for being reticent around the media even during the good times. Given the scrutiny he faced in the latter years of his career, he hardly could be blamed. During McGwire's three years as the Cardinals' batting coach, if I wanted to talk to him about Cardinals' hitters, he often obliged. But if I wanted to ask about his second career, he refused.

His second career had gone better than anyone could have expected, too. When Tony La Russa appointed McGwire to replace Hal McRae as the Cardinals hitting coach after the 2009 season, the consensus opinion was that La Russa was trying to help a friend get back in the game. Since his retirement in 2001, McGwire repeatedly had put off La Russa's offers to help out even on a limited basis during spring training.

But La Russa insisted he wanted McGwire because he felt he could do the job. La Russa had managed McGwire for virtually his entire 16-year playing career and had watched his transformation from raw slugger to accomplished hitter. He thought McGwire had a lot to offer professional hitters. La Russa even had sent a few Cardinals to Southern California to work with McGwire during the offseasons.

La Russa's belief in McGwire would be proven correct. Players raved about working with him, and during McGwire's three seasons as the Cardinals' hitting coach, the team posted the National League's best batting average and on-base percentage, tied the Colorado Rockies for most runs, and finished with the second fewest strikeouts.

McGwire had not shown to be anything close to a distraction at home or on the road. After his steroids admission with Bob Costas aired on MLB Network, McGwire did the interviews he had to do and by Opening

Day had pretty much succeeded in becoming yesterday's news.

His first public appearance in St. Louis since his retirement, however, would be major news. For nearly three months after he was hired, the Cardinals had said they would make McGwire available to the media. Finally, he was the one who suggested he appear at the team's Winter Warm-Up, an annual fan festival attended by thousands in a downtown St. Louis hotel during the middle of January. At the Warm-Up, he would be around those who had adored him when he was breaking home run records for the Cardinals from mid-1997 through 2001.

McGwire was given a long, thunderous ovation when he was introduced on center stage before a Q&A conducted by Cardinals radio announcer John Rooney. "I can't describe it," McGwire said later of the crowd's reaction. "My heart was beating fast, my stomach was turning. I didn't know what to expect. It was really cool."

After McGwire went in front of the fans, he met with a media contingent that included numerous national outlets that otherwise would not have been covering the Winter Warm-Up. That session was not so warm and fuzzy. Reporters had been told McGwire would answer questions in the same interview room where Cardinals players had been appearing for two days. But minutes before he was to talk, a switch was made. McGwire instead would talk in a hallway just outside of the interview room, a tiny area for such a large crowd.

Why the change? "Crowd and logistics," a Cardinals spokesman said, later admitting that the switch was a mistake. But by moving the presser, McGwire was afforded easy access to a side door that would allow him a quick and hassle-free exit. After just six minutes, spent mostly squirming and trying to dodge the most pointed questions, McGwire indeed slipped out surrounded by security.

His appearance with Costas had been a huge step in the right direction for McGwire and the Cardinals, but some of his answers had prompted more questions. McGwire, for example, had told Costas that his use of performance-enhancing drugs had nothing to do with him hitting 583 home runs. "I did it for health purposes," he told Costas.

This is a man whose integrity had been difficult to question until his regrettable testimony in 2005. McGwire had walked away from $30 million when he retired in 2001, choosing to end his career rather than hang on and collect a paycheck as his body and his bat continued to deteriorate. Yet even in his final two seasons, when injuries limited him to 89 and 97 games, McGwire managed to hit 32 and 29 homers, respectively.

When pressed about his reply that PEDs had not helped his power numbers, McGwire seemed to realize his explanation didn't jibe. But he would answer only, "I made a mistake," and taking steroids "was the biggest regret of my life." On his way out of the makeshift presser at the Winter Warm-Up, he made it clear he did not want to talk anymore about the topic. "I hope you all can accept this and let's all move on from this," he said.

While the frankness of at least a few of his answers could be questioned, the regret that McGwire displayed during his admission pressers was heartfelt and undeniable. He choked up several times during the Costas interview, particularly when he talked about the difficulty in admitting to his parents and La Russa that he had used performance-enhancers. McGwire said he had not told any of them until the day of his televised admission.

Considering the hit his reputation took because of his association with steroids, the manner in which McGwire has transitioned into his coaching career is nothing short of admirable and impressive. First in St. Louis and then in Los Angeles, where he took a job to be close to his family year-round, he has made the most of his second chance. Based on what he said in his return in 2013, the position is everything he thought it would be and more. "When I took the job in 2010, Tony said it's the hardest job in sports," McGwire said. "I have to agree. It's not an easy job to deal with everybody's personality, everybody's swing. You have to learn everybody, get to know who they are. The thing about hitting is that there is never a time when everybody is feeling good. There's always somebody feeling not good. I'm spending more time at the ballpark as a coach now than I did as a player because there's so much studying to do, so much studying of the pitchers, so much studying of the hitters."

But, good for him, there's nothing else he'd rather be doing. "It's something I love. It's in my blood," McGwire said. "I'm glad I accepted the job in 2010 and hope I'm doing this til the day I die."

Molina's Mastery

Rookie right-hander Carlos Martinez was understandably amped when he went to the mound at Miller Park trying to close out the Milwaukee Brewers for his first career save. The Cardinals had gone ahead 7–6 in the top of the 10th inning after blowing a two-run lead in the ninth, and that came a day after they had dropped a 15-inning gut-wrencher in Colorado. With the season in its final 10 days and the Cincinnati Reds and Pittsburgh Pirates pushing hard, the situation was the biggest that Martinez, an excitable type even in calmer times, had faced in his young career.

His first pitch to Caleb Gindl was a 98 mph fastball outside. The second was the same thing.

This is hardly how the Cardinals wanted the inning to start. But Mike Matheny did not need to send out pitching coach Derek Lilliquist to calm down the young right-hander. As soon as ball two plunked into Yadier Molina's mitt, the Cardinals catcher was out of his crouch and on the way to the mound.

Molina put his right hand on Martinez's back. He turned him around and told him to slow down, throw strikes, and everything would be okay. He said this in Spanish and he might have included a few choice words to make sure he had the youngster's attention. Molina trotted back to the plate, took his position, and waited to see his pep talk pay off.

The next pitch was another 98 mph fastball, but this one caught the outside corner. Then came a 96 mph two-seamer that Gindl grounded to shortstop Pete Kozma. Martinez struck out Sean Halton on four pitches and retired Jeff Bianchi on a grounder to third. Game over. No runs, no hits, no errors. Eight of Martinez's final 10 pitches were strikes.

And the legend of Yadier Molina had added another chapter. "People are always asking what makes [Molina] so valuable besides the statistics," Matheny said after that game. "There's no category for what he did right there. He just continues to do things to help us win that amaze all of us."

Exactly what had Molina said to Martinez? According to Molina, it was nothing magical. Something along the lines of just focus on one pitch at a time and do your job. Martinez echoed that. I asked Matheny about it again several days later, and he said that he wished he could have been on the mound to listen. The manager was joking, but his point was serious: he could learn from Molina, too.

Every Cardinals pitcher over the past decade appreciates what Molina means behind the plate. After every good start, Shelby Miller never failed to credit Molina for his guidance. As rookie after rookie debuted in 2013, each one talked about how awed they had been to throw to Molina. Lance Lynn remembers being a minor leaguer in big league spring training when Molina was assigned for the first time to catch his bullpen session. Lynn never had pitched above Double A, but Molina knew all about the youngster and his pitching arsenal. "A lot of times when a catcher hasn't caught you, they'll come out and be like, what do you want to throw?" Lynn said. "He comes out and goes throw this, this, and this. I'm like, okay. He'd never caught me, but he already knew what kind of pitcher I was. To take time like that for a kid like me shows you what kind of catcher and teammate he is."

There is little doubt these days about what kind of catcher Molina is. He is regarded as the best in the business with the accolades and the

Between his fielding and his ability to handle pitchers, Yadier Molina is incomparable behind the plate.

statistics to show for it. Molina has won seven consecutive Gold Gloves and has been voted the National League's overall best defender three times. In his 11 seasons in the majors, Molina has thrown out 44.8 percent of would-be base stealers, easily the highest percentage among regular catchers. Since his debut in 2004, opponents have stolen 317 bases against Molina. By comparison, two other catchers who have caught more than 1,000 games in that span, A.J. Pierzynski and Brian McCann, have allowed 821 and 691, respectively.

Molina also has been credited with picking off 52 runners, more than twice as many as any other catcher. He is considered among the best at framing pitches, and his 3.67 catchers' ERA is third best in the majors since 2004. But baseball has yet to come up with a system to measure his most valuable assets, the intangibles. If stats were available to measure the effectiveness of pitch calling, the ability to control a pitcher's tempo, and the presence of a catcher to instill confidence in his teammates, Molina would be considered even more superior. He probably would have won the Most Valuable Player award in 2013 instead of finishing third.

No less an authority than Hall of Fame manager Tony La Russa has called Molina the best catcher he has seen in his 50-plus years in professional baseball. And that was before Molina became a dangerous hitter. Matheny has told Cardinals fans they are watching the best catcher in major league history. At least once a season, he tells reporters about the first time he saw Molina catch and how he went home and told his wife that he wouldn't be staying with the Cardinals much longer. Indeed Molina replaced Matheny as the team's No. 1 catcher after 2004, even though Matheny had won three Gold Gloves for St. Louis. "When you are okay with letting a guy like Mike Matheny leave because you have Yadier coming up, that shows you how talented Yadier is," pitcher Adam Wainwright said.

Molina comes by his baseball talent honestly. He grew up in a baseball family in Puerto Rico, where his dad, Benjamin Molina, was a local legend for his playing and coaching. On the day that older brothers Bengie and Jose were winning a World Series title for the Angels in 2002, Yadier was at home watching Benjamin be inducted into Puerto Rico's Hall of Fame.

Benjamin died in 2007 when he suffered a heart attack on the baseball field across the street from his home. From the time his youngest son was old enough to walk, Yadier Molina says his dad took him to the ballpark just about every day. "I was just running around, having fun,"

Yadier told me after his father's death. "That really helped me be where I am right now. Sometimes kids spend more time on the computer and more time watching TV. Then you don't feel the love for the game like I did when I was young. My family taught me to be in love with baseball."

Jose was the first star of the family and was drafted by the Chicago Cubs in 1993. Bengie was signed by the Angels as an undrafted free agent after their mom, Gladys Molina, requested a scout, who was there to see Jose, also check out Bengie. By the time Yadier reached his teens, the family knew he would be the best of the bunch. He played on the highest level youth teams, and his teams were the ones that regularly traveled to the United States for tournaments. Yadier played third base and pitched mostly until he went into high school. By then his older brothers were nearing the majors, and Yadi said, "When I see they would be catching in the big leagues, I want to be just like them."

Both Jose and Bengie had made the majors when the Cardinals drafted Yadier in the fourth round in the 2000 draft. He didn't take long to impress his new team. Dave Ricketts, the club's renowned catcher instructor, was "raving about Yadi almost from Day One," said John Vuch, a longtime executive with the Cardinals. "It really hit everybody how good he was the year he played at Double A in 2003…At that point we realized this guy was not just good for a minor league catcher—he's really good overall. And not just with the catching, receiving, and throwing. We knew he could do all that, but what impressed that year was the cerebral side of the game."

Molina reached St. Louis the next year, and before long, the incumbent Matheny was scoping out teams that might be shopping for a catcher. Matheny held onto his job until Game 4 of the World Series, when, with the Cardinals a loss away from being swept, La Russa recognized the end of one tenure and the beginning of a new era by starting Molina. Though only 22, Molina did not let the spotlight of the World Series intimidate him. He went 0-for-2 before being lifted for a pinch-hitter in the 3–0 loss but still managed to make his presence felt. Red Sox slugger Manny Ramirez, who would be the series MVP, was at the plate, and Molina thought the slugger was peeking in to check the signs. Molina gave Ramirez a few words that made sure the Red Sox superstar knew such antics would not be tolerated. "At that age to have the nerve to get up and do that to a guy like that in the World Series showed you something," Wainwright said. Since Wainwright went into the rotation, only the battery of Cole Hamels and Carlos Ruiz in Philadelphia has worked together in more games.

Since Albert Pujols' departure, Molina has become the fan favorite at Busch Stadium, drawing the loudest cheers during introductions and ranking No. 1 on the team—and usually top five in the majors—in jersey sales. Still, as revered as he is in St. Louis, he remains a bigger hero in his homeland. When Edwin Rodriguez was named the manager of Puerto Rico in the 2013 World Baseball Classic, he told me the first call he made was to Molina. First, he wanted to be sure he would play. Second, he wanted Molina's input on who else to put on the team. "I was texting or calling him almost every day, asking for his help in putting together the team," Rodriguez said.

After Molina led Puerto Rico to its surprising second-place finish, Rodriguez had an even greater appreciation for Molina. "Besides the physical ability, which is obvious, his ability to study hitters is so impressive. I say that is his greatest strength as a catcher," Rodriguez said. The Puerto Rico manager recalled an at-bat during the WBC when Molina called for inside fastball after inside fastball instead of the soft stuff away that had been discussed pregame. "I looked over at my pitching coach like, what's going on," Rodriguez said. "Then Yadi looked into the dugout and nodded, like I've got this. Sure enough, the batter ended up striking out."

Molina has been regarded as such a superior defensive catcher since he reported in 2004, that the Cardinals never worried about his offense.

La Russa once said that Molina would be his catcher if he didn't get a hit all season. Molina almost scoffs at the notion that he wouldn't be a productive hitter. "When I came up, there was so much to do with getting to know the pitchers and getting them used to working with me that I did not even think about hitting," Molina once told me.

Since hitting only .216 in 2006, Molina has not finished a season below .262, and over the past four seasons, his batting average is .307. Through much of the first half of 2013, he led the National League in batting average and after dealing with a knee injury early in the second half he still finished the season with career bests in average at .319 and RBIs with 80. No less a hitting authority than Charlie Manuel in 2013 called Molina the most improved hitter he had seen in his nine years managing the Phillies and also the best catcher in the league.

Wacha! Wacha!

A high chopper that bounced just over Michael Wacha on the night of September 24 instantly became one of the Cardinals' most memorable images of 2013. One out from completing a no-hitter, the 6'6" Wacha was unable to get his glove quite high enough to snag the hit by Ryan Zimmerman. Wacha was denied a chance to make history but nonetheless had delivered one of the Cardinals' most unforgettable performances of the season and provided a hint at what he would do in the postseason that soon followed.

Yet his late-season gem against the Washington Nationals was not the most memorable outing of Wacha's regular season. At least not to anyone who had witnessed his major league debut against the Kansas City Royals on May 30 and stayed from start to finish. Anyone who stuck out that game will not likely forget it.

There, though, weren't many who stayed until the end. Based on estimates from the press box, less than 200 fans from a crowd of 43,916 remained inside Busch Stadium when Cardinals right fielder Carlos Beltran hit a grounder to first base for the final out—at 3:14 AM on Friday morning. Seven hours and 59 minutes after Wacha had been scheduled to throw the first pitch on Thursday night, the game finally had been completed.

Wacha showed little difficulty exceeding the lofty expectations that accompanied him to St. Louis for his debut. He had been drafted out of Texas A&M less than a year earlier with the 19th selection in the first round, a compensatory pick the Cardinals were awarded after Albert Pujols left for the Los Angeles Angels. Wacha had impressed the club in his first spring training and had been dominating for Triple A Memphis when he was called to the majors. The day before he made his debut, Wacha was asked if he believed he was in St. Louis to stay. That was the plan, he answered.

Such confidence was well founded, considering the way he pitched against Kansas City. Wacha did not allow a base runner in six of the seven innings he pitched and gave up just one run on two hits in the fifth inning. Wacha did not walk a batter, struck out six, and left with a 2–1 lead. Yet by the end of the affair, his first start would be overshadowed by so much else that happened on a wild night (and morning).

Right-handed reliever Mitchell Boggs would remember the game as the last he would pitch for the Cardinals. A career year as the club's top set-up man in 2012 had earned Boggs a spot on Team U.S.A. in the 2013 World Baseball Classic as well as a chance to close after Jason Motte was injured in spring training. But Boggs pitched so poorly early in the season that he was sent to the minors. He had returned the previous week but continued to struggle.

With his bullpen short-handed, Mike Matheny didn't have much choice but to send out Boggs to protect a one-run lead in the ninth inning. It took two pitches for the big Georgian to lose the lead. Pinch-hitter Jeff Francoeur, who was hitting .217 with one homer, knocked an

0–1 slider over the left-field fence to tie the game. After walking Alex Gordon, Boggs' night and Cardinals career were over. He was sent back to Memphis the next day and traded to the Colorado Rockies for cash considerations six weeks later.

Victor Marte relieved Boggs and fared just as poorly. He hit Alcides Escobar with his first pitch, and on his second, Marte made an errant throw after fielding a comebacker from David Lough. Now the bases were loaded, and still there were no outs. Eric Hosmer followed with a two-run double down the right-field line that give Kansas City a 4–2 lead.

Then the night turned crazy.

It was 10:32, and torrential rain started to fall. And it fell and it fell. The game had been delayed for an hour before it started because of weather, but that would be nothing compared to this stoppage. One hour passed, two hours passed, and the rain kept coming down. Under normal circumstances the game could have been suspended. But because this was the last time the interleague rivals were scheduled to meet that season and a new rule had been put in place, umpires were directed to make every effort to play the game in its entirety. If the game had been called, the score would have reverted back to the end of the eighth inning, and the Cardinals would have had a 2–1 victory.

The Royals would not have wanted that any time, of course, but especially now. This was before the Royals became the team that would win the 2014 American League pennant. These Royals had lost 12 of their past 13 games, including eight in a row, and had fallen into last place in the American League Central. Manager Ned Yost's job security was shaky. Earlier in the day, the Royals had shaken up their coaching staff by bringing franchise icon and Hall of Famer George Brett out of the executive office and making him the interim batting coach. Kansas City was downright desperate for a victory.

But the rulebook would have wiped out their chance to beat the Cardinals. According to Rule 4.12(b)(4), if a game was called while an inning was in progress during which the visiting team had taken the lead and the home team had not batted, the score would be reverted back to the last completed inning. The eighth had ended with the Cardinals in the lead.

When the rain finally subsided, less-than-ideal field conditions still had to be considered before play could resume. The Cardinals felt the health of their players would be at risk on such a slippery field. The Royals, not surprisingly, felt the groundskeepers could make it playable.

To be waiting for a game to resume at 2:00 AM inside a nearly empty ballpark made for a strange scene. What was transpiring outside the dugouts was even more unusual. On the visitors' side of the field, Yost and general manager Dayton Moore had ventured onto the playing surface to survey the situation. Several Royals players also had come out of the clubhouse and were assisting the grounds crew. On the home side, Matheny and his general manager, John Mozeliak, were doing their own inspections. Both GMs were plugged into their mobile phones, stating their cases to major league headquarters in New York.

Finally, at 3:04 AM, after a delay of four hours and 32 minutes, play resumed. Ten minutes later the game and Kansas City's losing streak were over. The Royals, who would not arrive in Texas until well after sunrise for that night's game against the Rangers, did not appear to be very tired. They also were quick to credit umpire "Cowboy" Joe West, the crew chief, with an assist for ending their losing streak. "I told the guys no more yelling at Joe West," said Francoeur, who has hit only one home run since that night. "He stuck it out for us. We have to thank him for that." Added Yost, "That wouldn't be fair for us to come back and just lose because it started raining. Joe West did a great job of giving us an opportunity."

A few minutes before 4 AM, West and the rest of his crew could be seen stepping into a limo outside of Busch Stadium. They were on their way to Chicago where they were scheduled to call a game at Wrigley Field in less than 10 hours.

Though Wacha's night had ended five hours before the game was over, he still was hanging out in the Cardinals' clubhouse at 3:30 to answer questions about his debut. "Definitely one to remember," he said. "I'll never forget this day, that's for sure. Even if I wasn't pitching, I'm not used to playing too many ballgames at 2:30 in the morning."

Wacha eventually would become much more familiar with weather issues. Of his first 12 starts in 2014, he would have to wait out at least one delay in five of them. Against the New York Yankees on May 26, his start was delayed for 61 minutes, though rain was still falling when the game started. "I didn't understand why we started the game when it was pouring down rain," he said. "It didn't affect me; I was just a little confused."

There's really not much that seems to affect or confuse Wacha when he is on the mound. On the night of September 24, 2013, with the Cardinals hot and heavy in a pennant race, the tall Texan certainly was not bothered by Washington. The Nationals had arrived in St. Louis as the hottest team in the National League, but they proved no match for the 22-year-old rookie.

Wacha was making just his ninth start and still trying to secure a place in the Cardinals' postseason pitching plans. With just five days in the regular season remaining, this would be his last chance. The Cardinals had sent Wacha to Memphis in the middle of the season, in part to save some of his innings for the stretch drive and partly to refine his curveball. Their plan was working better than they could have hoped. When Wacha returned to the rotation in early September, he did not allow a run in his first 17 innings over three starts. Wacha would pitch even better in his next start.

Turning in one of the team's best pitching performances in recent memory, Wacha left no doubt that he warranted another start in 2013. As his fastball touched 97 mph and his change-up baffled the Washington hitters, Wacha retired the first 14 Nationals he faced. Second baseman

Matt Carpenter botched a grounder to end the perfect game bid with two outs in the fifth, but Wacha got Wilson Ramos on a lineout and followed that with a three-up, three-down sixth. He walked Zimmerman to lead off the seventh and Adam LaRoche to start the eighth, but neither runner made it to second base. Shane Robinson, playing left field for injured Matt Holliday, preserved the no-hitter with a running catch near the foul line on a line drive by Anthony Rendon that ended the eighth.

Wacha went into the ninth having thrown 99 pitches, his second highest pitch total to that point. He got pinch-hitter Steve Lombardozzi on a ground-out to short for the first out and froze Denard Span with a full-count change-up for the second. Now he was an out away from the Cardinals' first no-hitter since 2001 when rookie lefty Bud Smith frustrated the San Diego Padres. On Wacha's first pitch to Zimmerman, a 97 mph fastball, the Nationals' third baseman knocked it to the ground about 10 feet in front of the plate where it took a high bounce. If Wacha were an inch taller or his glove an inch longer, he would have been able to snag the ball with plenty of time to throw to first. Instead, the ball ticked his glove, landed just beyond the mound, and was rolling toward second base when shortstop Pete Kozma made a bare-hand scoop and fired to first. His throw was in time but drew Matt Adams off the base. Adams swung around his glove toward Zimmerman but was too late. The no-hitter would not be. "Once I saw it get into his bare hand, I thought we had a pretty good chance that we were going to see an unbelievable finish to an unbelievable game," Matheny said.

The next day Wacha said he didn't want to think about what might have happened if Zimmerman's hit had not nicked his glove. "Thinking back on it, it was an incredible night," he said. Little did he know there would be even more incredible nights to come in October.

Young Guns

When Trevor Rosenthal struck out Adam LaRoche to close out a 4–1 victory against the Washington Nationals on September 25, 2013, he completed the Cardinals' most impressive pitching performance of the season. That is quite a statement, considering that one night earlier, Michael Wacha came within a two-outs-in-the-ninth-inning infield single from pitching a no-hitter, and earlier in the season, Shelby Miller came within a leadoff single of a perfect game.

But this performance wasn't about only one pitcher. This effort was a testament to a season-long rookie movement in St. Louis that culminated on this last Wednesday night of the regular season. To complete a three-game sweep of the Nationals, Mike Matheny called on five pitchers, and all five were rookies. All five had enjoyed exceptional seasons, and all five were in fine form on this night.

It started with Miller, the 22-year-old Texas fireballer. He allowed one run in six innings and would earn his 15th win, the most in the majors for a rookie. After giving up a one-out, run-scoring single to Bryce Harper in the first inning, Miller did not allow a runner to reach scoring position before departing after a leadoff walk in the seventh.

Seth Maness was the first of the rookies to follow, and on his second pitch, the "double-play guy" lived up to his nickname. Maness threw a sinker, his specialty, and Wilson Ramos grounded it to Daniel Descalso to trigger a 5-4-3 double play. It was the 15th double play opponents had grounded into against Maness since his debut in early May. He would induce another one three days later to finish the regular season with 16, tops among all National League relievers.

Lanky left-hander Kevin Siegrist entered in the eighth to face a couple of lefty hitters and he allowed a single to Denard Span after retiring Scott Hairston on a pop-up. This night was nothing special for Siegrist, but his season was historic. After being promoted in early June, Siegrist allowed only two runs in 45 outings, good for a 0.45 ERA. That was the lowest in the majors since 1911 for any pitcher who worked at least 35 innings.

Carlos "Baby Pedro" Martinez followed Siegrist and retired two of the Nationals' most dangerous hitters, Ryan Zimmerman and Jayson Werth, without issue. Martinez, who had turned 22 four days earlier, was beginning to settle into a late-inning role that he would handle through the Cardinals' postseason run. Martinez made a team-high 12 appearances in the playoffs and allowed runs in only three of them.

The ninth belonged to the hard-throwing Rosenthal, who secured his third save of the series with a three-up, three-down inning that included strikeouts of Harper and LaRoche. Rosenthal would finish the regular season with 75⅓ innings pitched and 108 strikeouts, third most among National League relievers. He would pitch even better in the postseason, working 11⅔ innings without being charged a run.

The fact that the youngsters recorded all 27 outs while allowing only five hits was not all that was notable about this night. Two points made it even more impressive. First, all five pitchers had been acquired and developed by the Cardinals. Also, each of the five threw at least 96 mph with the exception of Maness, and his sinker is so effective it might as well be a trick pitch. And the kicker: each guy except Maness came in throwing harder than the guy he replaced.

Miller topped out at 96 mph, Siegrist touched 97, Martinez got up to "only" 99 in this game, and Rosenthal reached 100 on the pitch before he fooled LaRoche with a 90 mph change-up in the dirt. If this wasn't the first time a team had four pitchers top 95 mph in the same game, it must have been the first time a team had four rookie pitchers throw that hard in one night. "You give them opportunities and then you can't deny the talent," Matheny said. "We saw some young guys with very good talent, and they're letting it shine."

Youngsters had been making the most of their opportunities all season. In all, the Cardinals called on 12 rookie pitchers in 2013, and half of them spent more than half the season in St. Louis. Six of the team's 12 pitchers on the World Series roster were rookies. Rookies handled 38.5 percent of the team's pitching workload in 2013, including playoffs. They combined for a 3.08 ERA, and their 36 wins were the most collected by rookies on the same team in the majors.

Although the Cardinals had not anticipated such a major contribution from their rookies in 2013, the arrival of so many young arms in one year hardly was a coincidence. The onset of all the 20-something pitchers was the result of two plans that had been put in place years earlier. In 2003, even though the Cardinals had made the playoffs for three straight seasons, club chairman Bill DeWitt Jr. directed the front office to start focusing less on free agents and trades and more on drafting and developing players. He was tired of seeing the Cardinals' farm system finish in the bottom tier of the industry's organizational rankings. DeWitt also sensed a change coming to the game that would allow small-market teams to be better-equipped financially to hang onto their star players rather than unload them as their salaries rose and they approached free-agent status. "We really didn't have a good farm system," DeWitt explained to me in 2013 during an interview after *USA TODAY* had named the Cardinals the No. 1 franchise in the major leagues. "We were ranked 25th to 30th pretty regularly and rightfully so. We didn't have a lot coming. We knew we couldn't continue to get free agents or get players from clubs that were trying to move payroll. That game was ending. We felt the best way to compete longer term was to put our resources in acquiring our own players and developing them."

DeWitt in 2003 had hired Jeff Luhnow, an analytical whiz he knew through other business. The hiring was questioned by the established front office because Luhnow had no background in baseball. Other than the ability to speak Spanish fluently, he seemed to lack the qualifications for his first position with the Cardinals, which was to beef up the club's player-procurement efforts in the Dominican Republic and Venezuela.

Just two years later, Luhnow had impressed ownership enough that he was given far greater responsibility. He was named the director of amateur scouting and given the authority to implement greater use of analytics in the process of evaluating prospects. Luhnow was promoted again in 2006 when DeWitt named him vice president of scouting and player development.

Luhnow's rapid rise did not sit well with the general manager at the time, Walt Jocketty. Though highly respected throughout baseball, Jocketty was a traditionalist. He had climbed to his position through old-school scouting and did not endorse the extensive use of computer-generated data in evaluating players. Following a period of growing disharmony in the front office, DeWitt fired Jocketty at the end of the 2007 season.

Around this time, the Cardinals also started to look differently at pitching talent. The club began to focus more on a prospect's athleticism and arm strength than his amateur accomplishments. After years of favoring college pitchers over high school pitchers in the draft, where the prospects came from no longer factored in. Finding big arms became the priority. By 2009 many of the changes had taken hold. "It was still an evolution going on, but around '09 was when we felt we had everything up and running and a process in place that we were comfortable with," said general manager John Mozeliak, who had succeeded Jocketty.

The onslaught of rookies to arrive in 2013 validated the changed approach, in part because of the varied approaches they used to reach St. Louis. Only one of the 12—Maikel Cleto—had not originally signed with the Cardinals. Miller and Wacha were prototypical, big time pitching prospects from a state known for producing big arms. Both were taken with the 19th pick in the first round of their respective drafts, Miller in 2009 out of Brownwood (Texas) High School and Wacha in 2012 out of Texas A&M. While Wacha zipped through the system and debuted less than a year after he had been drafted, Miller encountered the bumps that typically accompany high school picks. At one point when he was pitching in the minors in 2012, the club was so concerned with his stubbornness to do things his way that they implemented a "no-shake" rule. Miller was told to throw whatever pitch the catcher called—rather than shake off the backstop's signal.

Martinez took a much different journey to reach the majors. He grew up playing shortstop in the Dominican Republic, and the six-foot-tall hurler lacked the stature of the 6'4" Miller and 6'6" Wacha. But Martinez was long on athleticism and threw a fastball well into the 90-mph range. Martinez also had run afoul of Major League Baseball. After he signed with the Boston Red Sox as an under-the-radar 17-year-old by the name of Carlos Matias, MLB's standard background check uncovered inconsistencies in his age and true name. Less than a month after he signed in February 2009, the contract was voided, and MLB ruled that Martinez could not sign another contract for a year.

This suspension, believe it or not, would make Martinez a lot of money. He continued to work out, but he no longer was under the radar. Interest from other clubs soared like the velocity on his fastball, which was rising into the upper-90s. In the meantime MLB determined that Martinez had not set out to deceive anyone. His birth name indeed was Matias, but he chose the Martinez name after an uncle who raised him, following the death of Carlos' mother. Any discrepancies in his age were regarded as minor.

By the time the suspension was lifted, Martinez was viewed as a first-round talent except he was not subjected to the draft. He could sign with whatever team he chose. He chose the Cardinals, who gave him a $1.5 million signing bonus just 13 months after the Red Sox thought they had secured his services for $160,000.

Rosenthal epitomized the Cardinals' new approach to drafting pitchers. He had not been drafted out of Lee's Summit West High School near Kansas City and had gone to Cowley (Kansas) County Community

College to play shortstop and third base. In a postseason tournament after his freshman year, however, he made a brief appearance on the mound that was seen by Cardinals scout Aaron Looper. Rosenthal showed both of the qualities the Cardinals now coveted. He was athletic enough to play shortstop, and his fastball reached 95 mph.

Knowing he had not been heavily scouted by other teams, the Cardinals did not draft Rosenthal until the 21st round in 2009. He climbed through the minors at a steady but not spectacular pace until 2012. That year he skipped high Single A, spent three months starting at Double A, and was promoted to Triple A. After only three starts with the Memphis Redbirds, the Cardinals promoted Rosenthal on July 16 to bolster their bullpen. By October he had emerged as one of their most valuable relievers.

Siegrist rose from even greater obscurity to reach the majors. He wasn't drafted until the 41st round—the 1,235th pick overall—in 2008 after an undistinguished season at Palm Beach Community College. The Cardinals took a flyer mainly because the 6'5", 200-pounder looked like a pitcher and he threw left-handed. For a long time, Siegrist battled injuries and gave little indication that he ever would become a shutdown reliever in the majors. He spent time at all seven stops in the system and was still languishing as a starter in Class A four years after being drafted. But the Cardinals made him a full-time reliever in spring training 2013, and he took off. Barely two months into the 2013 season, Siegrist was pitching in St. Louis.

Maness' road to the big leagues was not quite as circuitous. He had been a standout in high school in Pinehurst, North Carolina, and then at East Carolina University. Maness was drafted by the Florida Marlins in the 41st round in 2010, but he decided he'd be better off returning to East Carolina for his senior year. The decision paid off. In 2011 he was taken 30 rounds earlier by the Cardinals.

Although Maness lacks a big time fastball, an uncanny ability to throw strikes put him on a fast track to St. Louis. As a starter in Single and Double A in 2012, he struck out 112 and walked only 10 in 169⅔ innings and was named the organization's Minor League Pitcher of the Year. Maness began 2013 as a starter at Memphis but was promoted to the big leagues just a few weeks into the season when the Cardinals shook up their bullpen. In his first outing, Maness retired all three batters on groundouts and the next day induced his first double play. When a potential rally needed snuffing, he quickly became Matheny's go-to reliever.

Finding the talent is only the first step. It must also be developed, and the Cardinals have long been known as one of baseball's best organizations in preparing players for the majors. "It's not just by chance," said Matheny, who served as a roving instructor in the minor leagues before he became the manager.

What is the key to their success of grooming prospects? It starts with finding the right guys. "Character plays a lot into how we draft," said Adam Wainwright, who has served as mentor for many of the youngsters. "You're drafting on talent plus intangibles. These guys all have those intangibles that make them good professionals."

"They all have great stuff, but they also have real good heads," pitcher Chris Carpenter said. "They listen, they learn, they pay attention to the guys who have been here. When you learn in that atmosphere, you have a great chance to succeed."

To be given a consistent message helps, too, and the Cardinals teach the same way in rookie ball as they do in the majors. When a player is drafted by the Cardinals, he can expect a couple of packages: a team warm-up jacket and an 86-page book titled the *Cardinal Way*. The jacket helps everyone look like they're on the same team. The book ensures that every player is given a consistent message about how to play. The mantra, according to Matheny, is "work ahead in the count, stay low in the strike zone, do not be afraid to challenge hitters, and use your defense."

When a player is invited to big league camp, he is treated like more than the wide-eyed new kid on the block. Matheny sets up the practice drills by mixing veteran players with young players in the same group. This might seem like a small and rather obvious practice, but it is not universal. "In a lot of organizations, they group veterans with veterans and rookies with rookies," said Bryan Eversgerd, a Cardinals minor league pitching coach who is given the opportunity to work with major league coaches in the spring. "Mike mixes them up. That way a guy like Wacha gets to rub elbows with the veterans so when he gets to St. Louis, it's not like they're strangers. That first day in the big leagues can be overwhelming. To already know the veteran guys gives the young guy a certain level of comfort that can be really important."

The rookies pay attention, too. They follow the veterans like little puppies. Even in the lunch room, they are watching. Maness, for example, learned that Wainwright eats the same type of food before every start so that he knows how his body will feel when he makes his way to the mound. "He knows what it takes to stay here. So you pay attention," Maness said. "Everybody up here has the ability, but it's microscopic things like that that separate the weak."

Having the right players to emulate is vital and the Cardinals' veterans take their leadership responsibilities seriously. Carpenter was there to mentor Wainwright, who is now there for all the newcomers. When a pitcher arrives in St. Louis, he can count on a meeting with Wainwright. The message Wainwright offers the rookies is not anything secret. He tells them to be themselves and continue to do what they've been doing. After all, that's how they reached the big leagues. When Wacha was sent down to the minors in his first spring training, Wainwright asked, "So what are you going to do now?"

Wacha's reply: "I don't know."

"Just keep doing what you're doing," Wainwright told Wacha. "You did great."

When Wacha was called up, he heard the same question.

"This time he knew," Wainwright said. "So far, they've all given me the right answer."

When Wainwright was called up for the first time in 2005, he didn't experience such a fostering atmosphere. Rookies were expected not only to stay quiet, but also to stay away from the veterans. Wainwright learned this the hard way. He was sitting down to watch some of the starters play a video game in the clubhouse when one of them turned around and voiced his displeasure for all to hear. "He got all over me for just watching. I wasn't playing," Wainwright said. "Then the whole clubhouse joined in with the 'who do you think you are' stuff. Sometimes that stuff went overboard."

As the young guns found out in 2014, sustaining success in the majors is even more difficult than getting there. Virtually all of the 2013 rookies struggled at times in 2014, and three already have been shipped out of St. Louis. Still, the best should still be ahead for all of them. "These guys are 22, 23 years old. It's so impressive to see them up there and what they're doing," Wainwright said. "When I was that age, I was nowhere near ready compared to these guys."

Wainwright: A Georgia Pitch

Adam Wainwright did not want to let go. He had just pitched the Cardinals into the 2013 National League Championship Series with a 6–1 complete-game victory against the Pittsburgh Pirates and—as his teammates gathered around to celebrate—he continued to hug his catcher. This had been the biggest performance of his career, and he wanted to share the moment with his longtime battery mate, Yadier Molina, for as long as possible. Their hug following the 2006 World Series clincher had not been quite what Wainwright wanted. "I give him heck because we got a quick hug in, and then he kind of shoved me out

The ace of the Cardinals, Adam Wainwright (50), embraces catcher Yadier Molina after defeating the Pittsburgh Pirates in Game 5 of the 2013 NLDS.

of the way and went after Albert for a big hug," Wainwright said. "I told him I wasn't going to let him go the next time we got to do that. And I didn't." He added, "There was nobody else I wanted to share that moment with more than Yadi Molina."

In a five-game series that had been full of memorable moments, none were any cooler than the one at the top of the ninth. When Wainwright made the fastest sprint of his career from the dugout to the mound to try and get the final three outs, the sold-out crowd at Busch Stadium gave him a roar that left him with "chill bumps from my head to my toes." Manager Mike Matheny felt it, too. "That made my hair stand up," Matheny said.

Through eight innings, the 6'7" right-hander had dominated the Pirates. He allowed more than one base runner in an inning only once, the seventh, when the Pirates came up with three infield singles that all could have been outs. The last of the grounders hit first base, bounced over Matt Adams, and brought home Pittsburgh's only score. But other than that inning, Wainwright shut down the Pirates with a fastball regularly reaching 95 mph and a curve that his catcher called "amazing." "I was calling it more than usual because it was breaking so good," Molina said.

All six of Wainwright's strikeouts ended with his signature pitch, including the final out of the game when slugger Pedro Alvarez swung and missed at three in a row. After Wainwright beat the Pirates in Game 1, their hitters had talked about staying off the curve and making him beat them with his fastball. One problem there. "I can throw [curves] for strikes," Wainwright said. "If I get them in my counts, eventually they're going to have to start swinging and be aggressive."

As Wainwright stood amidst the clubhouse celebration surrounded by reporters, Chris Carpenter walked up and poured a cold beer over the head of his longtime teammate and close friend. "I don't waste a lot of beers," Carpenter said. "But he deserves it." Said Wainwright: "I'm trying to live up to the standard he put out to be that Cardinal leader. That's the guy I've always wanted to be watching Carp. I knew someday it was going to be my time to step up and fulfill that."

Adam Parrish Wainwright was born in Brunswick, Georgia, and raised in the tourist community located on the coast in the southeastern corner of the state. Wainwright calls it paradise, the kind of slice of Americana where Norman Rockwell would have found many scenes to his liking. One of them would have been the parade from the pier to the park on the Opening Day of the youth baseball season. "Some of my best memories of growing up were opening day of little league," Wainwright said. "We'd have pizza catered for everyone and snow cones and a baseball card show." Recalled his mom, Nancy Wainwright: "The whole community lines the street and claps for the kids as they come by. Adam grew up with everybody being supportive and people hanging out at the ballpark. It was a real genuine family atmosphere."

The next best thing to playing baseball for Adam was watching baseball, specifically Atlanta Braves baseball. He spent many summer suppers in front of a TV with his older brother, Trey, rooting on Greg Maddux, Tom Glavine, and—Adam's favorite—John Smoltz. By the time Adam entered high school, his dream of playing professional baseball began to look like an obtainable goal. If he could play for the Braves, his dream really would come true. They were the first team to scout him and actually saw him shine as a kicker and receiver in football before they saw him pitch. From 10th grade on, the Braves scouted Adam more closely than any team.

A sore arm kept Adam from pitching in showcase events the summer following his junior year at Glynn Academy yet he entered his senior year thinking he had a chance to be drafted as high as the third round in the 2000 draft. As his senior year progressed and he started hearing from more scouts, the second round felt like a possibility. As his fastball kept improving—he was touching 95 mph by end of senior year—Adam's stock continued to rise. At the Georgia high school All-Star Game two weeks before the draft, he made another step toward the first round. "I started throwing a slider that day," Adam said. "The scouts were like, 'Whoa, okay, we have something here.'"

The Braves owned two picks late in the first round, at 29 and 30, and Rob English, the Braves' area scout who had followed Adam, was starting to believe that Wainwright would not last that long. Adam said the Toronto Blue Jays, who had the 18th pick, were the other team besides the Braves that he thought was most interested. Two days before the draft, however, the Pirates flew him to Pittsburgh and worked him out as a right fielder. "I loved to hit. I mean I loved to hit," said Wainwright, rattling off stats from his school. "My freshman year I hit .333, my sophomore year I hit .400 on the nose, junior year .500, and senior year .515, with like six, nine, and nine home runs. And I knew if a team signed me to hit and it didn't work out, I could go pitch."

Whatever team that drafted Wainwright would be dealing with a

family affair. Trey was attending law school at Georgia Tech and looking to someday become a sports agent. He would serve as Adam's advisor, negotiating his signing bonus and, before that, doing what he could
to enhance his younger brother's chances of being picked by the Braves.

As Adam's stock rose in the days before the draft, the Wainwrights
began to hear from numerous teams. They wanted to know much it would
take to sign him. He had committed to a scholarship at Georgia Tech so
teams knew he would not be an easy sign. If Adam would agree to terms
beforehand, some teams would be far more willing to draft him if he was
available. The more the phone rang, the more difficult Trey figured his
job would be of steering his brother to the home-state team. Trey came
to the conclusion that Adam had out-pitched the Braves' 29th pick.

The Wainwrights were thinking $1 million. If Trey told a team what
it would take to sign Adam, the chances of him falling to the Braves
would decrease. If Trey told teams the Wainwrights didn't want a
pre-draft agreement, teams were more likely to back off. Though the
Wainwrights knew the Braves were interested, the family had no way to
know what the team really wanted to do. On the day before the draft,
Trey reached out to English. "Rob, this is getting very interesting," Trey
recalled from the conversation. "We're getting a lot of teams asking if
Adam is going to sign for X amount if they take him in the first round.
These are teams that would be interested if he agreed to a number. Do
you know what the Braves are thinking? Is there any assurance you can
give us if he gets to 29 what the Braves will do? If there is, we'll tell these
teams we're not interested in doing a pre-draft deal."

English checked with his front office, called Trey, and told him the
Braves had only a couple of players ranked higher that Adam. Though
the Braves expected Adam to be taken among the first 10 picks, English
could not make any promises to the Wainwrights. But Trey did not need
absolute assurance. He sensed from his conversation with English that
Atlanta would choose Adam if he was available at 29. That was enough

for Trey. He told the teams picking ahead of the Braves that they were going to let the draft play out. There would be no deals beforehand.

On the next day, surrounded by a few hundred of their closest friends and neighbors, the Wainwrights gathered around a computer to follow the draft and keep their fingers crossed that Adam would end up with his favorite team. "Sure enough, when they got to the 29th pick, it was 'the Atlanta Braves select ID number 0997, Wainwright, Adam, pitcher from Brunswick Georgia,'" Trey said. "We all went nuts. We had an opportunity to steer him in a different direction and did not. It worked out that he fell to where he wanted to."

For Trey, the fun had just begun. The aspiring lawyer, who had interned the previous summer for an Atlanta-based sports agency, would handle the negotiations for his younger brother's signing bonus. First step: Trey pulled out several years worth of *Baseball America*, an industry standard in covering the draft. "We decided as a family that we could do this," Trey said. "We've got the information and we've got the knowledge. Let's get Adam through the draft and sign, then he can spend a lot of time figuring out who would be the best agent for him." (Eventually he hired Steve Hammonds, who remains his agent.)

Adam was drafted on a Monday, and the Braves sent assistant general manager Dayton Moore to the Wainwrights' home on Thursday. Trey made what Moore remembered was a convincing argument for Adam. Though Moore was impressed, the Braves' offer did not change. It wasn't the $1 million Trey had in mind, not by a long shot. Moore had driven from Atlanta with the plan of staying one day but ended up spending the night. The two went back and forth the next day before Moore told Trey that he wasn't authorized to make any further offers and went out to his car. It still wasn't quite as much as Trey had in mind.

Trey did not want Adam to accept the offer and actually told his younger brother to wait in the other room while he handled the talks. When Moore went out to his car, Adam was growing impatient. He told

Trey he was ready to sign. "Basically, he said that it was enough for him," Trey said. Trey went out to inform Moore, who returned to the house ready to make a deal. The Wainwrights did not yet know that Moore had gained approval to up the offer by $250,000. When they heard of the increased offer, Trey said, "Adam beamed." He was set to begin his professional career with a $1.25 million signing bonus, which was in line with what players drafted in front of him received. Older brother had played hardball against the big leagues and done all right.

Three-plus years later, Wainwright would have a day even more memorable than when he was drafted or signed. Wainwright had gone to the home of Jenny Curry, his girlfriend at the time, to ask her father, Jim Curry, if he could marry his daughter. The small talk was almost over, and Adam was warming up to pop the question, but his cell phone would not stop buzzing. Finally, he turned it off. Then the Currys' home phone rang, and Jim went to answer it. The call was for Adam. His mom was calling to tell him the Braves needed to talk to him. He had been traded to the Cardinals, and the teams didn't want him to hear the news on TV. "My mom was crying," Adam said. "The whole city was crying. It turned out to be one of the greatest moments of my life. He acknowledged that I could marry his daughter, which was great."

Ten years and two World Series championships later, Wainwright signed what he hopes will make him a Cardinal for life: a five-year, $97.5 million contract extension. He could have waited until after the 2013 season to become a free agent and after the success he had—leading the majors in innings and the National League in wins (19)—Wainwright would have been poised to land millions and millions more. But he might have had to leave the Cardinals. "I said to Adam, 'I can't even fathom those kids of numbers,'" Nancy Wainwright said. "He said, Mom, 'I can't either. The thing I'm the proudest of is I'm going to start and finish my career as a St. Louis Cardinal.' He was more interested in securing his future for his family and for himself than the dollar amount."

What has helped make Wainwright one of baseball's best-paid starters is a curveball that has been considered one of the game's best since late October of 2006. The breaking pitch has defied conventional thinking in more than one way. The rule of thumb for throwing a curve: don't try it until you're old enough to shave. Such reasoning is sound. Until you hit puberty, your arm is not developed enough to handle the stress required to snap off a curve.

Good thing for the Cardinals that Adam Wainwright did not pay attention to the time-honored, if unwritten, rule. The man who throws what is widely regarded as the best curve in the business started throwing it before he turned 10 years old. Blame—well, credit—Trey for turning his back on little league protocol. Because their parents were divorced and their dad moved away, Trey served as Adam's mentor and coach when they were growing up. Trey was a pretty fair high school pitcher and often used his younger brother as a catch partner in the backyard. If young Adam had to catch a curve thrown by someone seven years his senior, Trey at least could show him how to throw one.

Not only did Adam learn the curve when he was allegedly too young, but because Trey is a left-hander, Adam was taught how to grip it backward. He claims he's never changed his grip either. So the keys to throwing a knee-buckling curve is learning it as a preteen and using an unconventional grip? Absolutely says Adam, who believes the earlier you start throwing the pitch, the better it will be. "These kids who don't throw their breaking ball until they are in high school, their breaking ball is going to stink," Adam said. "You have to develop that just like you would any other pitch. It's a pitch that has so much feel involved, it's hard to develop."

Besides, nobody truly knows if throwing curves at an early age had anything to do with Adam requiring Tommy John surgery in 2011. After all, he had been spinning pitches for nearly 20 years. Similarly, nobody can be sure if throwing so many curves led to a bout of elbow tendinitis that cost Wainwright an early-season start in 2014 and resulted in offseason surgery. At this point, as Adam acknowledged, what does it matter? "Would you want me to stop throwing my curveball," Wainwright said, in a tone that made it clear that he has no such intentions.

Adam spent countless hours developing the feel for his curve on a mound throwing into a backstop that Trey had constructed in their backyard. The mound is long gone, but Nancy says the backstop remains. "They still always look to make sure," Nancy said.

Wainwright was called up by the Cardinals for the first time at the end of the 2005 season and made the team as a reliever in '06. By the end of the season, with closer Jason Isringhausen dealing with a bad hip, the rookie right-hander took over the closer's role for a team headed to the playoffs. Wainwright had all of five saves in his career when he threw the most famous curveball in Cardinals' history.

The pitch ended a classic, seven-game National League Championship Series against the New York Mets and sent the Cardinals to the World Series. Molina had just given the Cardinals a 3–1 lead in the top of the ninth with a two-run homer when Tony La Russa called on Wainwright for the final three outs. Wainwright didn't make it easy. He gave up singles to the seventh and eighth hitters in the Mets lineup—Jose Valentin and Endy Chavez—before striking out pinch-hitter Cliff Floyd for the first out. Jose Reyes lined to center for out No. 2 before Wainwright walked Paul Lo Duca to bring up the Mets' most dangerous hitter, Carlos Beltran.

Two postseasons earlier with the Houston Astros, Beltran almost singlehandedly defeated the Cardinals in the NLCS by scoring 12 runs, hitting four homers, and reaching base 18 times before Jim Edmonds' heroics pulled out a seven-game victory for the Cardinals. Now Beltran was facing a 25-year-old rookie with the bases loaded and the season on the line for both teams. Before the curve, though, came a change-up. A change-up and a change in plans, that is. Before Beltran batted, Molina went out to talk to Wainwright about what to throw on the first pitch, and they decided to go with a sinker down and away. On the way back to the plate, Molina changed his mind. He called for a change-up, a pitch that Wainwright rarely threw. "Think about that," Wainwright said. "I'm [25] years old, greener than he is by a lot, and he only has a year. It's Game 7, bases loaded, Beltran's up, and I maybe had thrown 10 change-ups all year."

Molina had concluded that Beltran would be waiting for a fastball so a change might catch him off-balance. Wainwright went with his catcher's instinct. "Beltran was almost certainly looking dead red right there," Wainwright said. The location wasn't great—"thigh high down the middle," according to Wainwright—but the pitch selection was superb. Beltran took it for strike one. "He looked out at me, like, 'Did you just throw me a change-up?'" Wainwright said. "The bases are loaded, and on your first pitch, you throw me your fourth-best pitch. Did you really just do that?"

Beltran fouled off the next pitch and then, with his bat stuck on his shoulder, he watched the curve that put the Cardinals in the World Series. The first pitch, said Wainwright, had set up the entire at-bat. It would go a long way in defining his career, too. "If I give up a hit right there on the change-up, they score two runs at least," Wainwright said. "Maybe he hits a home run, and I'm getting run out of St. Louis. I could be coaching high school baseball right now."

Trey was back in Georgia for what was then the biggest moment of his little brother's career. While in college and law school, Trey had driven all over Georgia and its neighboring states to watch Adam play football, soccer, and baseball. With pitch clicker in hand, he rarely had missed a game Adam pitched at any level. Now that Adam was in the biggest situation of his career, Trey would have to watch on TV. His wedding anniversary would take priority. "I was struggling back and forth that day about whether to fly to New York, but I decided to stay home and spend the evening with my wife—albeit a baseball evening. There was no doubt we would be watching that game," Trey said.

95

By the bottom of the ninth, the game already had produced a season's worth of drama. Anyone who has watched a family member in a pressure situation can relate to what Trey was feeling. "Watching Adam in that moment, I was as nervous as I had ever been in my whole life. I was incredibly stressed out," Trey said. "When he struck out Carlos Beltran, I was screaming and jumping up and down and crying. It really was an outpouring of every emotion…[It also was] "The last time I missed a game like that."

Eight years later, Trey was in the clubhouse after Adam's gem in Game 5 of the National League Division Series against the Pirates. As soon as Adam finished his postgame interviews, he walked over to Trey and gave him a long hug.

A Boston Bummer

Boston is a wonderful place to visit, but the Cardinals haven't enjoyed their recent travels there. Not in October, anyway. Of course, it's not much fun when you have played five World Series games at Fenway Park since 2004 and lost four of them. But losing has been only part of their difficulty. Their actual travels to Beantown were no more enjoyable than watching David Ortiz demolish their pitching in 2013.

In 2004 a hotel downtown could not be found for the visiting team in the World Series so the Cardinals had to hole up in nearby Quincy. Nothing against the fine Irish suburb, but its postgame dining options are limited and it did not offer much for the Cardinals' families to do during the day. When you reach the World Series, you'd think you'd warrant staying in the cool part of town. But because the Head of the Charles regatta was held the same weekend as Games 1 and 2, downtown was booked. Instead of staying within sight of Fenway, the Cardinals were an $80 cab ride away. Tony La Russa did not hide his disappointment. "For most of these guys, this is their first World Series experience,"

La Russa told the *St. Louis Post-Dispatch*. "When the game is over, if you're [in Boston] there are all kind of restaurants. In Quincy, there wasn't anything except for the hotel that stayed open for us. We shouldn't have had this problem."

Not surprisingly, Quincy did not take kindly to the manager's remarks. Mayor William Phelan said his town's restaurants stayed open plenty late for the townsfolk. "If St. Louis had a decent pitching staff, they would have been back in Quincy in plenty of time to visit any one of our 30 fantastic restaurants," the mayor told his local newspaper, *The Quincy Patriot-Ledger*.

Where the Cardinals stayed had nothing to do with being swept by the Red Sox. Chris Carpenter was out, and Matt Morris was pitching at considerably less than 100 percent (He admitted it the following spring and told me he would do so again if it was the World Series.) Besides, once the Boston Red Sox completed their historic comeback against the New York Yankees, they seemed destined to end their 86-year drought without winning the World Series. As future Hall of Famer, Pedro Martinez has said—after rallying from three games down in the American League Championship Series—no way the Red Sox were going to lose in the next round.

The Cardinals' accommodations at the downtown Sheraton were first class in 2013. It was perhaps a mile from Fenway and with fine dining in every direction and plenty of nearby spots to take the children. The problem was getting to the hotel. Rather than fly back to Boston immediately after Game 5 in St. Louis, the Cardinals opted for another night at home and to travel on the off day before Game 6. If all had gone as scheduled, they would have arrived in Boston before dark and had the evening to relax. But the schedule was thrown *way* off by a mechanical issue with the team's Delta charter flight.

The Cardinals ended up spending most of their off day on the runway at Lambert-St. Louis International Airport. The plane was loaded with players, families, and club staffers and preparing to depart when an issue was found with the navigation systems. For an hour and a half, mechanics tried unsuccessfully to correct the problem. That plane was ruled out, and another had to be located and flown to St. Louis. The faulty plane had to be unloaded, and the substitute had to be loaded.

By the time the Cardinals left St. Louis, it was 9:00 PM, seven hours later than they had been scheduled to depart. The team buses pulled up to the hotel shortly before midnight with a couple of dozen passersby milling outside and numerous reporters inside to check on the state of the team. The players weren't in much of a mood for media, and Mike Matheny did his best to cut off the interviews. He couldn't really be blamed for wanting his team to be left alone at the end of such a long day.

Throughout the ordeal the travel party had held up better than one would expect, considering a dozen kids were among those who spent seven hours on one plane before having to pile into another one. "The mood was amazingly positive," general manager John Mozeliak told mlb.com at the hotel. "The young children on this flight were awesome. Everybody involved decided to take the patient trail and deal with it. In the end it was unfortunate, but we were there for a reason and we're happy to be there." Players such as David Freese and Matt Carpenter went to Twitter to keep Cardinals Nation updated throughout the day and evening. Tweeted Carpenter: "On the bright side really getting to know some of my teammates' children."

Even the afternoon press conferences that had been scheduled for Matheny and the next game's starter, Michael Wacha, went on as planned. Though the delay was only a couple of hours old at this point, everyone seemed to be making the best of a trying situation. "Everybody seems to be doing all right," said Matheny via a teleconference while waiting for the flight. "We have some younger kids, but I'm impressed with how everybody has handled it. Fortunately we have plenty of food, snacks for the kids, lots of entertainment with on-board movies, and everybody travels with all their high-tech stuff. Most of these kids are pretty happy that they're not in school right now, and no complaints so far." Said Wacha: "Everyone is just watching movies. They've got dinner on here for us, and everyone is just walking around. Nobody is in a bad mood or anything like that."

The Cardinals would not be in such a good mood the next night when Shane Victorino broke a 0–0 tie with a two-out, bases-loaded double in the third inning that gave the Red Sox a 3–0 lead and sent them on the way to a 6–1 victory for their third World Series championship since 2004, and two of them came at the expense of the Cardinals.

PART III:
2012

Cardinals Record: 88–74

Cardinals Finish: Won NLDS against Washington Nationals

Won Wild-Card against Atlanta Braves

A Cure for the Winter Blues

By the middle of January, St. Louis is ready for some baseball. Winter has taken hold, and Opening Day remains nearly two months away, but thanks to the Cardinals and St. Louis baseball writers, there is a chance to get close to the game. For three days every President Day's weekend, the Cardinals stage a wildly popular fan event called the Winter Warm-Up. It's staged not at Busch Stadium but at a nearby hotel. No game action is involved except what is shown on the video monitors.

But baseball, specifically Cardinals baseball, is all over the place. The Warm-Up is where Mark McGwire made his first public appearance before he returned to the Cardinals as hitting coach in 2010. It's where Carlos Beltran was introduced as a Cardinal in 2012 and where so many other newcomers have first felt the love from St. Louis fans. It's where Cardinals past and present sign autographs, club executives interact with fans, memorabilia is peddled, and, from the time the doors open at 9:00 until they close at 5:00, a sea of red crowded shoulder to shoulder slowly roams through the Hyatt Regency St. Louis at the Arch.

Attendance is not cheap with an admission of $40 for everyone 10 and older, but the proceeds benefit a good cause. We're talking about a lot of proceeds, too. Since the first Warm-Up was held in 1997, more than $18 million has been raised for Cardinals Care, the club's charitable arm. Autograph signings generate much of the revenue and also provide a fascinating study of the players' popularity. Present Cardinals are expected, if not required, by the club to attend on one of the three days, and for some of the younger players, participation in one of the regional touring Cardinal Caravans also is mandatory.

Players typically sign autographs for an hour at a price set by the team, and that cost displays the unofficial but market-driven popularity scale. In 2014 an Adam Wainwright autograph was the most expensive to buy at $80, but that amount was less than half of the $175 that an Albert Pujols signature fetched in his final four years with the Cardinals.

Despite that lofty price, tickets for Pujols sold out the quickest, too. Yadier Molina was priced at $100 in 2014, but, in what has become somewhat of a Warm-Up tradition, he did not attend.

Matt Holliday went for $100 in 2011 but had dropped to $75 by 2014. Michael Wacha, on the other hand, jumped from $5 in 2013 to $70 in the 2014 Warm-Up, following his breakout October. David Freese had an even greater one-year increase, going from $5 to $75 following his dream postseason. Matt Carpenter cost $40 in 2014 just two years after being free. Jon Jay, meanwhile, has been a model of consistency. In 2014 his autograph was priced at $20 for the third straight year.

The Warm-Up is not the only place to see the Cardinals during the weekend. Many of the players also attend a dinner program staged by the St. Louis chapter of the Baseball Writers' Association of America. In a reflection of the decline in baseball's popularity over the years, St. Louis remains one of only three chapters—New York and Boston are the others—that continues to host an annual dinner. The main purpose of the event is to recognize Cardinals achievements from the previous season and honor past players and teams. But great entertainment is part of the menu, too.

In 2014, for example, the 1964 Cardinals were recognized in the 50th anniversary of their seven-game World Series victory against the New York Yankees. As part of the program, five players from that team hosted a Q&A for fans at center stage. To hear Bob Gibson, Tim McCarver, Bob Uecker, Dick Groat, and Mike Shannon reflect on the championship season not only was a chance to relive history but also good for several laughs. Of course, whenever the self-deprecating Uecker speaks at a public function, it is a time for laughter. When he was introduced, he deadpanned, "I remember a big part of the World Series for me was the Cardinals wanted to make a move. They wanted to play Dal Maxvill and asked me to take an injection of hepatitis so they could make that roster move."

Gibson was the only one of the five ex-Cardinals who wasn't still working as a baseball broadcaster of some sort. He had tried the gig, too, after he retired but found part of the job not to his liking. "Being a broadcaster is a lot like being a politician," Gibson told the crowd. "You have to lie a lot. I had a problem with that. My career wasn't going to last long because they don't want you to tell the truth that often."

As much enjoyment as the 1964 Cardinals generated for the audience in 2014, they did not outdo Lance Berkman at the 2012 Baseball Writers' dinner. That was a momentous event to begin with because the Cardinals were coming off their 2011 World Series championship, and Tony La Russa was being recognized for his retirement. The only reason Berkman did not steal the show was because La Russa also was entertaining. Hearing Berkman tell a few stories, however, was a highlight. He was there because his teammates had voted him the winner of the club's 2011 Darryl Kile Award, which recognizes a Cardinals player who best exemplifies being a "good teammate, great friend and fine father, and a humble man."

Though Berkman had been with the club for only one season, the impact he made on his teammates had been that strong. Previous Kile Award winner Matt Holliday introduced Berkman, a player known as a great storyteller. "I'm going to make this short because I'm pretty sure Lance is going to talk for a while," Holliday said. Not much could brighten the mood of the club more than a tale from Berkman in his Texas twang. As you listened to Berkman accept the award, you quickly understood what Holliday was talking about. He was appropriately respectful and genuinely touched in accepting the award. He had not known Kile, but one of his closest friends on the Houston Astros, Jeff Bagwell, had been extremely tight with the right-hander. Kile had spent his first seven major league seasons with Houston. After the pitcher died in a Chicago hotel room on a Cardinals road trip in 2002, Berkman said, "Baggie really wasn't the same after that happened. It had a huge impact on him."

As the crowd grew somber, Berkman said it was time to lighten the mood. To do so, he said he would tell one of his "A-list" stories, an anecdote he brings out only when he's talking to a crowd of more than 700. He was playing left field for the Rice University Owls at Texas Christian in Fort Worth when a 35 mph or so wind blew straight across the field. TCU had sent up a left-handed pinch-hitter during the late innings of a close game, and the hitter drove a ball to what Berkman thought was going to be left-center. Berkman took off toward center field only to see that the wind was carrying the ball in the opposite direction. "If y'all thought I wasn't a great outfielder this year, that was back when I was younger and hadn't learned anything yet," he said. "The harder I'm running, the faster the ball is being pushed to the foul line. I think I've got a bead on it. I dive for the ball and end up missing it by six inches."

Then the fun began. The ball rolled to the left-field foul pole, and Berkman hustled to the fence. When he arrived the ball was hidden. "I'm not kidding you, there was a bunch of debris like Big Mac containers, soda cans, and napkins," Berkman said. "I'm rooting around on my hands and knees for the ball, trying to find it. Meanwhile, this guy is circling them up." Berkman located the ball on the top of a plastic grocery bag and when he picked it up, he also grabbed the bag. "I'm on my knees and I can't throw the ball and the bag at the same time," Berkman said. He shook his hand to let loose of the bag, but the wind caught the bag just as Berkman made his throw. "I'm telling you, as soon as I let that sucker go, that bag whipped up right in front of me and I threw the ball straight into the plastic bag," Berkman said. "It goes like 10 feet maybe. I don't have a great arm, but that killed it."

By that time he also was stuck on the ground because his spikes had become entangled with the chain-link outfield fence. By the time he was able to get up and retrieve the ball, TCU had an inside-the-park home run, and Berkman's coach, Wayne Graham, was running out to left field.

"I started to say, 'Coach, I'm okay, I'll shake it off,'" Berkman said. "He says, 'I'm not out here to check on you...you're the worst outfielder I've seen in my life.' Then he turned around and ran back to the dugout." The laughter subsided, and Berkman went back to his seat. Interestingly, since his retirement following the 2013 season, Berkman has joined Graham's staff as a volunteer coach as he works to finish his degree at Rice.

Matheny Rules the Roost

Mike Matheny sat smiling in the visiting manager's office at Marlins Park. His dark hair was wet, and his undershirt clung to him. Minutes earlier, his players had administered not one but two cold water soakings as a reward for beginning his managerial career with a victory. The real prize, besides the W, was the gameball Matheny was showing off to owner Bill DeWitt Jr. and me. "Yadi had a big smile when he came up and gave it to me," said Matheny, obviously touched by the treatment from his players.

As the defending World Series champions, the Cardinals were chosen to open new Marlins Park against the newly named and new-look Miami Marlins. The home team had pulled out all the stops in the pregame festivities. It trotted out wildly dressed dancers to escort the Marlins, brought in Jose Feliciano to sing the national anthem, and invited Muhammad Ali to deliver the first pitch. The scene was spectacular, the park was packed, and the music was rocking.

But the Cardinals had spoiled the party with a convincing 4–1 victory. Kyle Lohse did not allow the Marlins a hit until the seventh inning, and David Freese, in his first at-bat since being named the MVP of the 2011 World Series, drove in two runs that put the Cardinals ahead early and for good. When Jason Motte struck out Giancarlo Stanton for the final out, the Matheny era was off to a winning start. "I was thinking about that all spring, getting that first one for Mike in this park in the season opener," Freese said. "That's what we wanted to do. It was a special night."

On hand was Matheny's predecessor Tony La Russa, who was watching his first game in his retirement following 33 years in the dugout. La Russa, serving in his new role as a Major League Baseball vice president, watched from the press box. Perhaps mindful of the unwritten "no cheering in the press box" rule, he clapped ever so softly when Matheny was introduced before the game. The Cardinals also were playing without Albert Pujols for the first time since 2000 and right-hander Chris Carpenter, who was dealing with a shoulder issue that soon enough would end his career. The Cardinals had entered spring training thinking that Carpenter would make the Opening Day start, but he would not pitch until September.

St. Louis did not miss a step without the terrific trio that had been so instrumental in the franchise's success for so many years. Credit Matheny for leading what would be a seamless transition from Hall of Fame skipper to rookie manager. The surprising decision to hire Matheny as La Russa's successor already was looking like the right one.

When La Russa stepped down after 16 years in St. Louis, the Cardinals had an appealing choice of potential successors. They could have gone with the manager who ended the Red Sox's 86-year drought of World Series championships, two-time champ Terry Francona. They could have opted for a Hall of Fame player, Ryne Sandberg, who had been paying dues for years in the minors. They could have stayed in-house and promoted Jose Oquendo, the longtime coach and fan favorite from his years playing with the Cardinals.

But the Cardinals decided to take a risk. To replace the winningest manager in franchise history, the Cardinals hired a 41-year-old who had not managed a day in his life unless you count his sons' youth league teams. Besides a lack of experience, Matheny possessed all the qualities that DeWitt and general manager John Mozeliak were seeking. He was a strong leader, which they knew from the five seasons he played for the Cardinals. The presence and personality he displayed during his interview had blown away the team's four-man interview panel that in addition to DeWitt and Mozeliak, included assistant general manager Michael Girsch, and special assistant Mike Jorgensen. "After that, we looked at each other and said, 'Wow, I don't think we can do any better than this,'" DeWitt said.

The brain trust learned something else about Matheny during the interview, too. He had been paying attention during his three-plus years as a special advisor with the club. Part of his role was to visit the club's minor league affiliates and assist the young players. While doing this Matheny also had watched and studied nearly every player in the organization. His familiarity with the up-and-comers gave him a clear advantage over the other candidates. "He knew who was coming. He knew where certain players might have an opportunity to do better. He hadn't been on the inside of discussions about any of our players, but he clearly had been doing his homework," DeWitt said. "He nailed that part of the interview."

During his 13 seasons as a catcher, Matheny had developed a reputation around baseball for leadership and toughness. His leadership usually was displayed behind closed doors, where Matheny had no problem getting in the face of a teammate if he felt there was a need. His toughness had become near legendary—for good reason. Matheny was forced to retire as a player because of concussions that left him, according to one friend, "not sure of his name for a year and a half." The majority of the concussions were believed to be a result of foul tips to the catcher's mask, but Matheny had been involved in his share of collisions at the plate, too, and he rarely had backed down. He wanted his teammates' respect and did whatever he could to gain it.

When Matheny left the Cardinals after the 2004 season, he signed a three-year deal with the San Francisco Giants. Hoping he could make

The 49th manager in Cardinals history, Mike Matheny walks out to the mound during Game 6 of the 2012 NLCS.

an impression on his new teammates, Matheny went on a paintball expedition with his fellow Giants in spring training one night, even though his wife, Kristin, had just arrived from St. Louis for a short visit. "It was a great opportunity for me to say, 'Guys, I'm going to dinner with my wife,'" Matheny says. "But I told her I really have to do this."

And did he ever impress his teammates. Near the end of the outing, enough pellets remained for a final round, which the players decided to make a battle to the last man standing. On one side were pitchers and catchers; on the other were position players. "They lined us up, and we took off running right at the opposing team," Matheny recalled. "All of a sudden, my hopper comes open, and all my paintballs fell out. I'm reaching for the ground, trying to put balls back in my gun. I end up getting reloaded and I took another guy's gun."

At this point with time running short, Matheny made like Arnold Schwarzenegger in *The Terminator*. With a paintball gun in each hand, he stood up and told the position players to bring it on. They did—and they did some more. "I'm just getting drilled, but I'm thinking I can't surrender," he said. "At the end, I was still standing. I hadn't quit."

And he had the welts to prove it. Instead of enjoying a dinner with her husband, Kristin spent the evening counting the marks left on him from the paintball pummeling. "My wife counted 180-some different times where I got hit," Matheny said. "I didn't think you could get a fever from welts, but I had one." His last-man stand, though, had accomplished what he had wanted. "It's amazing what an impact it had," Matheny said. "I had guys talk about that forever. I didn't think it was that big a deal. Everybody got shot—just some of us more than others."

More than five years later, at least one of those teammates still had not forgotten. I called Steve Finley, who played with the Giants for one season with Matheny, to see what he remembered about the last man standing. As soon as I told Finley I wanted to test his memory for a story about Matheny, his first words were, "Does this have anything to do with paintball?" Finley added, "That is one of the memories I have etched in my mind about Mike Matheny."

David Freese told me he was unfamiliar with that story, but someone had told him another one about his strong-jawed skipper. On May 26, 1998, Matheny was catching for the Milwaukee Brewers when he came up to bat in the bottom of the ninth with runners on first and second and his team trailing the Pittsburgh Pirates 2–1. Matheny, not known for his hitting, had been having even more trouble than usual with curveballs and was working hard to stay on the pitch. Even as he watched what he thought was a curve, he was determined to not bail out. Hard-throwing reliever Rich Loiselle, however, had thrown a fastball that was coming right at Matheny's face. Matheny did not bail on the pitch—and splat— the ball hit him square on the left side of his face, just above his mouth. He took a step back, put his bat on the ground, and placed his left hand on his hip. Somehow, he stayed on his feet even as catcher Jason Kendall and umpire Jerry Crawford quickly motioned to the bench for assistance. "Ninety-some miles per hour flush in the jaw, and he didn't even go down," Freese said, shaking his head in disbelief all those years later. "He was spitting out blood and he just walked to the dugout."

After the game, which the Brewers won 3–2 in large part because of the hit-by-pitch, Matheny approached a teammate and asked him, "Did I go down?"

He was told no.

"Good," Matheny replied.

Matheny escaped with four stitches in his mouth and the loss of a couple of teeth. From the hospital that night, he let Brewers manager Phil Garner know that he would be ready to play the next day. He did— all 10 innings—in fact.

That kind of toughness can set the tone for a clubhouse. "It trickles down for sure," Freese said. "As extremely tough as Mike is physically, mentally he overpowers his physical toughness. You just feel it when you're around him. You understand quickly how tough Mike is, the way he handles the good and the bad."

* * *

In Matheny's first three seasons, his players have defended and supported him without fail. But on June 23, 2013, that changed. Maybe a two-hour and 59-minute weather delay had something to do with fouling the mood. Or maybe being swept for the first time in 2013 brought out the unpleasantness. Whatever the reason, Adam Wainwright was downright steamed at his manager after the Cardinals lost 2–1 to the Texas Rangers. It hardly mattered that what bothered Wainwright was the kind of stuff that has been miffing starting pitchers for as long as managers have been taking them out of games.

The Cardinals led 1–0 in the top of the seventh, and Wainwright had retired the first two Rangers when trouble began. Texas right fielder David Murphy slammed a full-count curveball off the right-field wall, and No. 8 hitter Leonys Martin lined a single on the seventh pitch of his at-bat to drive in Murphy and tie the game. Matheny promptly pulled Wainwright, who also had allowed two base runners in the previous inning and had thrown 105 pitches. Not happy to be pulled, Wainwright undoubtedly grew more frustrated when Martin scored against reliever Trevor Rosenthal, and the Cardinals ended up losing. "Two pretty stressful innings in a row," Matheny explained about lifting Wainwright. "Adam was making good pitches all the way through. [Martin] kept fighting, ended up putting together a good enough at-bat to get the run across the plate. [Wainwright] did a great job for us today."

When Matheny was asked a second question about lifting his ace, he went on the defensive. A stern look on his face, he took a second to gather himself before he answered. "It is a tricky call," Matheny said.

"After he's labored, like we said, he's thrown over 20 pitches in that inning. We've got our eighth-inning guy, and Waino is going to be up second [in the bottom of the seventh]. He's not going to hit for himself. We've got an opportunity for [Rosenthal] to come in. He's going to pitch the next [inning], too. He can get one out and get us out of that, hopefully get us an opportunity to get a run."

Wainwright wasn't buying. Not for a second. Following Matheny's presser, the media went into the clubhouse for the pitcher's comments. When Wainwright was told that Matheny thought he had been laboring, you could almost see the anger rising in the usually affable hurler. "He's wrong. You don't want to call your manager out, and I would never do that," Wainwright said before doing just that. "Laboring is not what I was doing. He's the manager. He makes the call. If you think I'm laboring because I went into deep counts, I went into deep counts all day, made good pitches. That's his opinion."

Matheny was not happy when Wainwright's comments were relayed to him, but the manager blamed the media. We had set up Wainwright, he said. The potential was there for the club to be disrupted, but Wainwright would not let the disagreement fester.

Two days later, after an off day, Wainwright showed the respect he has for his manager by publicly apologizing for his comments. The Cardinals were in Houston when he called Bernie Miklasz, the lead columnist for the *St. Louis Post-Dispatch*, and asked for an outlet to clear the air. "I fell into compulsive and irrational anger and I hate that," Wainwright said, according to Miklasz's story. "I want to be a good leader and help set the tone for what the Cardinals stand for. I'm embarrassed by what I did. I will apologize to Mike personally when I see him today." Wainwright went on to praise his skipper. "Mike Matheny is my leader and one of my mentors in life," he said. "I love that man. I need to make it up to a guy I have as much respect for as anyone in the world. To put him in a hard position like that is unforgivable."

Kozma's Good Karma

The Cardinals were ready to pop. They had just completed a remarkable rally from a 6–0 deficit to beat the Washington Nationals in the decisive Game 5 of the 2012 National League Division Series, and it was time to cut loose. Players were circled around the icy tubs of adult beverages in the visitors' clubhouse at Nationals Park, waiting for Chris Carpenter to give them the go-ahead. But not everyone was present. Infielders Pete Kozma and Daniel Descalso remained on the field being interviewed after their ninth-inning hits had made the difference in the Cardinals' 9–7 victory.

Descalso entered the clubhouse after a couple of minutes and was cheered loudly, but there still was no sight of Kozma. Enough was enough, so Carpenter went to find the rookie shortstop and usher him to the celebration. Once Kozma had joined his teammates, Carpenter proclaimed, "Pete gets the first pop!"

For Carpenter to be toasting Kozma only added to the unlikeliness of the unprecedented comeback. Carpenter was the veteran ace and team leader. Kozma was the quiet rookie promoted barely a month earlier after he had hit just .232 for Memphis. But when Rafael Furcal injured his right elbow in late August, the Cardinals needed a shortstop, and Kozma was summoned. He responded by hitting .333 after his call-up and had slugged a three-run homer in the Cardinals' 8–0 victory in Game 3 against the Nationals.

But Nationals manager Davey Johnson was not impressed enough to order Kozma intentionally walked with the game on the line and Jason Motte due to bat next. The Cardinals reliever had not batted all season and had struck out in his only four big league plate appearances dating to 2009. While Mike Matheny could have pinch hit Tony Cruz, that would have meant the Nationals would not have had to face Motte in the bottom of the ninth.

Nationals bench coach Randy Knorr asked the Nationals manager whether he wanted to free pass Kozma. Johnson declined, and his reason for pitching to Kozma was not hard to defend. Closer Drew Storen already had walked two in the inning, and an intentional walk to Kozma would have loaded the bases. Storen would not have any margin for error.

Storen jumped ahead of Kozma with 94 and 95 mph sinkers that were called strikes but followed with two balls. Storen then made a grievous mistake. He threw another 94 mph sinker, but it stayed at waist level, and Kozma lined it to right field to score two runs and absolutely stun Nationals Park. The Cardinals had tallied four runs in the ninth with two outs and twice had been one strike from the end of their season.

After the incredible comeback, the calmest Cardinal in the clubhouse was the one who had held up the postgame champagne festivities. Asked what he was trying to do in the ninth, Kozma shrugged. "Get a hit," he said. He pointed to Descalso's single that had glanced off shortstop Ian Desmond's glove as the real key. "That took the edge off," Kozma said.

Give the Oklahoman props for staying true to himself. Since being called up on the last day of August, he had taken to heart the rookie code of "speak only when spoken to." Either that, or Kozma just didn't care much for conversation. He not only was quiet around the media, but he also didn't spend much time around his teammates away from the park either.

A timely hit against the Nationals wasn't going to change him even if this was a chance to gloat in front of all the fans who had considered the first-round pick a bust at the age of 24. Since being drafted in 2007, Kozma had spent six years in the minors with only two brief call-ups. Though considered strong defensively, Kozma struggled at the plate. His batting average in the minors for those years was .236. Perhaps Kozma didn't talk much to reporters because he understood how fleeting fame could be and he could be humbled as quickly as he had been hailed a hero.

Kozma's play in September and October would earn him the starting shortstop's job in 2013 when Furcal opted before the season to undergo elbow surgery that would sideline him for the year. Even at the end of his first full season in the majors, Kozma remained as unimpressed with his success as he would later seem unbothered about his shortcomings.

His personality proved ideal for his situation. After Kozma's dismal season at the plate in 2013—a .217/.275/.273 slash line—general manager John Mozeliak made it clear that finding an upgrade at shortstop would be a top priority for the offseason. When the club came to terms with Jhonny Peralta, Kozma quickly became the forgotten one. He said he did not hear from anyone on the club when it signed someone to take his job, adding that he didn't need to. Though a phone call or even a text would have been nice, Kozma said he was well aware of his performance.

Once the club acquired Peralta, Kozma faced the grim possibility of returning to the minors one year after being the starting shortstop for the National League champions. He spent most of the year in Memphis, too, though he started the season in the majors because of an injury to Mark Ellis and was jerked between the majors and minors a couple of other times. Kozma once was called up and sent down without even dressing out for the Cardinals.

But he persevered and improved his swing. Near the end of the minor league season, Kozma was called back to the big leagues. He would play so well in September that he would be named to the postseason roster ahead of Ellis. Through all of his ups and downs, Kozma remained as stoic as a statue. Shortly before the Cardinals departed for Los Angeles and the opening of the NLDS, Kozma had not been told if he would be one of the 25 players to suit up against the Dodgers. "No news is good news," he told me. He not only made the roster, Matheny put him into the lineup for Game 1, just as he had against the Dodgers in the NLCS the previous season.

Graceful Beltran and His Game 7 Woes

Carlos Beltran was rounding third base when his season ended in Game 7 of the 2012 National League Championship Series. Six years earlier, he had been standing in the batter's box when an Adam Wainwright curveball froze him with the bases loaded and his New York Mets down by two runs in Game 7 of the NLCS. And two years before that in 2004, Beltran was watching from the visitors' dugout at Busch Stadium as Jason Isringhausen closed out the Houston Astros in, yes, Game 7 of the NLCS.

Nobody knows close calls in October like Beltran. When the Cardinals blew their three-games-to-one lead against the San Francisco Giants in 2012, Beltran became the first player in major league history to play in three Game 7s without reaching the World Series. "It hurts because you get so close," Beltran told me months later.

But nobody handles that hurt with more dignity than Beltran—perhaps because he's had so much practice. More likely, he's just a true professional. "I don't want to say that it really hurts because someone has to win, someone has to lose," he said. "I've been part of the losing three times, but I feel so proud just to be in that situation. You know how many players do not have those opportunities. I don't feel bad at all." He even smiled at the notion that his Game 7 defeats have led to sleepless nights and countless hours of wondering what could have been. "It's something that really doesn't stay in my mind for very long," he said. "For me it's like, it's over, guys. We cannot rewind it. We have to think about next year."

Ah, next year. That would have been 2013, and, finally, after 16 seasons, Beltran would go to his first World Series. He didn't have to go through a Game 7 to win the NLCS either. The Cardinals pounded Clayton Kershaw and the Los Angeles Dodgers 9–0 in Game 6. Yet in the postgame jubilation, Beltran appeared as cool as ever. When the victory had been secured, Beltran jogged onto the field, hugged his teammates, and started with the interviews. A few minutes later, he sought

Carlos Beltran displays his smooth swing during June of 2012, though he would once again fail to reach the World Series that year.

out his wife, Jessica, gathered his two daughters, and joined his teammates for the trophy presentation.

He wore a smile that stretched from ear to ear but acted as calm as he had in the third inning when he smoked a 94 mph fastball into right field to drive in Matt Carpenter for the Cardinals' first run. "He's the smoothest man I've ever met," Wainwright said, "as cool as the under side of the pillow."

Jessica, though, knew better. She knew that her husband had been as jumpy the night before the decisive game as a 16-year-old on a first date. She had woken in the middle of the night, turned over, and saw her husband lying on his back, fully awake, pretending to be holding a baseball bat. "What are you doing," she asked. "He was like, 'I'm practicing my grip.'"

Jessica added, "I think it paid off, right?"

More than a little. Beltran not only drove in the game's first run, but he also finished with three hits, two RBIs, and a highlight catch in right field. In the best win of his life, he had been a difference-maker. It all started with his middle-of-the-night vision. "I'm thinking about the game, thinking about what I need to do, and envisioning in my mind having success," Beltran said. "You can't sleep in the playoffs. I think about the game, I envision myself having success before it happens. Hopefully, all the positive you put into your brain, you think about it and hopefully you can come through."

After driving in the first run in the third, Beltran drove in the Cardinals' final run with a two-out single in the fifth. With the victory virtually secured, Mike Matheny pulled Beltran in the eighth to allow him to enjoy the final outs from the dugout. "It's a dream come true," he said. "I'm thinking about how hard I have fought through my career. I think about my family, my dad, my mom. I think about my people, my country, my town where I grew up. Everybody there has helped me to be who I am right now. I know they feel proud and it's a great feeling."

An hour after the game ended, Beltran still was holding court inside the champagne-drenched clubhouse, showing his usual patience and professionalism with the media. A few feet away, Jessica was watching the celebration with a special eye on her husband. "He hasn't stopped smiling," she said.

To have the chance to smile like that in October was why Beltran had come to the Cardinals. The Mets did not make it back to the playoffs with Beltran, and in the final months of his contract, New York traded him to San Francisco for the 2011 stretch run. The Giants were in first place when they acquired Beltran, but they lost eight of their first 10 games with him, and he injured his right hand and went on the disabled list. The Giants never got it going again, finished eight games out, and did not show much interest in bringing back Beltran.

Plenty of other teams were interested in his services. Beltran wasn't sure about the Cardinals, at least not early in the free-agent process. But on the final day of the 2011 Winter Meetings, the Angels made Albert Pujols a $254 million offer, and just like that, the Cardinals' interest in Beltran went from uncertain to sizzling. Within two weeks of losing Pujols, the Cardinals had signed Beltran to a two-year, $26 million deal. "When I made my list of teams after the season, St. Louis was on the list," Beltran said. "But I didn't know if Pujols was going to leave. When he ended up leaving, I felt the chances of being able to go to the Cardinals would increase. It happened that way and pretty fast."

The Cardinals were more than a little familiar with the switch-hitting outfielder—in part from their encounters in the 2004 and 2006 NLCS. In those two seven-game series, Beltran bashed St. Louis pitching at a .353 clip with seven homers, 20 runs, and a 1.280 on-base plus slugging percentage (OPS). But such highlights came fewer and farther between after 2006. Issues with both knees limited Beltran to a total of 145 games in 2009 and 2010 before he bounced back in 2011 by hitting .300, making the All-Star team, and playing in 142 games.

Lance Berkman had played alongside Beltran with the Astros in 2004 and knew what kind of player the Cardinals had added. "He runs pretty out there," said Berkman, teasing but still accurate. "He's got a great way about him, a grace that will handle center field very, very well."

Beltran, 34 when he signed with St. Louis, did not play much center field with the Cardinals, but he still proved to be an ideal fit from Day One. He singled in his first at-bat and scored the Cardinals' first run of the 2012 season, helping them disappoint the Miami Marlins in the opening of their new stadium. Midway through June, Beltran was hitting .301 and leading the National League with 19 homers. He slumped in July and August but still finished with 32 homers—the most on the team—played in 151 games, and hit .269. Beltran didn't slip much if any the following season either, when he hit .296 with 24 homers and again was named to the National League All-Star team.

On as well as off the field, Beltran went about his business in St. Louis with a poise and purpose not often seen in professional athletics. Part of his smoothness was an athleticism that helped him become the first switch-hitter in history to hit more than 300 homers and steal more than 300 bases. But more goes into that grace than natural ability. Beltran is a proponent of what he calls the "80 percent approach." By always playing under such control, the game doesn't speed up on him. In a key time, he doesn't try to get ahead of himself. He always seems to be in the right place at the right time. "When you do things at 100 percent, you're out of control," Beltran explained. "So I live life at 80 percent and I can control my life the right way. I try to be as relaxed as I can be because that's something that works for me."

The bigger the situation, the better it seems to work. Consider Beltran's stats in the postseason. He has a 1.128 OPS that ranks behind only Babe Ruth and Lou Gehrig among players with at least 100 plate appearances in the postseason. Beltran's .333 batting average is tops among active players. In his first trip to the playoffs with Houston in

2004, Beltran homered in five consecutive games, hit .435, and scored a record 21 runs in only 12 games. His manager at the time, Phil Garner, has yet to see a performance to match it. "He hammered just about every ball you can hammer. He took three balls that were probably six inches off the ground and just rifled them right out of the ballpark," Garner said. "He hit them so far and hard he made them look like John Daly cranking on a golf ball in those days. You would be hard-pressed to find anybody who hit the ball as hard and as consistently as he did that year."

Said Beltran: "It was incredible. I went out, and good things happened for me. I didn't go out, thinking I need to do this or that to help the team. I told myself, enjoy it because you never know as a ballplayer when you're going to have this opportunity again."

That's about as much of an explanation for his playoff excellence that Beltran will offer. He admits that his concentration with every pitch becomes so great that he is mentally exhausted after playoff games. "It's not like you take playing for granted during the season, but because it's every day, it's hard to keep that kind of focus," he said.

Wouldn't you know it? After waiting 16 seasons to reach the World Series, Beltran was injured on the very first ball hit to him. It was the second inning of the first game, and the Cardinals already were losing 4–0. The Red Sox had the bases loaded with David Ortiz at bat, and he lofted a fastball that looked like it was going to land in the Red Sox bullpen for a grand slam. But Beltran rushed back, stretched out his glove arm, and caught the ball as his right side banged into the padded fence. He would have to leave the game before he batted again, and his status for the rest of the series would be day to day.

Before Game 3 Beltran received the Roberto Clemente Award, which recognizes the player who best represents the game on and off the field. Beltran had opened a baseball academy in his Puerto Rico homeland that combined education with teaching the game. Earlier in 2013, the academy graduated its first class—43 seniors who had earned college scholarships or been selected in the amateur draft. The graduation had been scheduled on a Cardinals off day so Beltran could attend. Far more than a benefactor, Beltran spends much of his offseason at the school. "When I'm at home, I'm at the school every day," he said. "If there is a kid not doing good in academics, I call him in my office. I want him to do things the right way, but I want to be a friend. I want them to be happy. That is my main priority."

With the assistance of pain shots, Beltran managed to play in the remaining games and he even reached base in all of them. Still, he was not close to 100 percent. But just as he had driven in the Cardinals' first run in his first game with the team, he also drove in their final run in his final game with St. Louis. His RBI single in the seventh inning of Game 6 was the only run the Cardinals scored in the Red Sox's clinching 6–1 victory.

Because the visitors' clubhouse at Fenway Park is not much bigger than a pitcher's mound, Beltran did his postgame media scrum in an open area where he barely could be heard above the celebration. Reporters from New York, St. Louis, and all over the land wanted to hear him address his future as well as the present. "At the end of the day, we all want to win," he said. "We battled to get to this point, but we didn't play good baseball. That's not the team that we know we can be."

He added, "Honestly, I'm not disappointed. I had a blast, man. Not only this year but last year, too. I made a good choice to sign with this organization. When I look around at the new friendships I built in this organization, I feel proud. They gave me an opportunity to play in the postseason and in my position, that's what you're looking for. You want to have the opportunity to win a World Series. This year we got here. At the end of the day, I am satisfied."

PART IV:
2011

Cardinals Record: 90–72

*Cardinals Finish: Won World Series
against Texas Rangers*

Won NLCS against Milwaukee Brewers

Won NLDS against Philadelphia Phillies

Holliday Overcomes Weird Injuries

Matt Holliday was primed for a banner 2011. He was coming off a 2010 season during which he hit .312 with 103 RBIs. He had enjoyed a strong spring training and gone 3-for-4 with a home run on Opening Day. But shortly after he drove home from Busch Stadium, the minor discomfort Holliday had felt in his lower abdomen was becoming rather major. When the pain didn't let up, Holliday headed to the hospital. He underwent an appendectomy the next day.

And a season full of bizarre mishaps had just begun.

Though Holliday was expected to miss up to four weeks because of the procedure, he was back in the lineup 10 days later and reached base three times. He continued to hit through April and May, and his batting average reached a lofty .394 on May 14. But two weeks later, Holliday landed on the disabled list with a strained quadriceps, which would turn out to his most "normal" injury of the season. Again, he returned with a bang and blasted a home run in his first game back after 15 days on the disabled list. The next month, Holliday missed a game because of food poisoning, and two weeks after that, he strained his back working out in the Busch Stadium weight room, and that cost him two games.

By September, when he hurt a finger swinging a bat in the on-deck circle, all he could do was shrug. That injury kept him out of the lineup for 11 days and eventually came back to plague him in the classic Game 6 of the World Series. Holliday had reached on an error and advanced to third base where he represented the go-ahead run with one out. But he was picked off by Texas Rangers catcher Mike Napoli, who rifled a throw to third baseman Adrian Beltre. Holliday dove back to the base but was unable to reach safely because Beltre's foot blocked the base. Holliday was nailed. On the next pitch, Rangers reliever Alexi Ogando unleashed a wild pitch to the backstop that would have allowed Holliday to score. Adding injury to embarrassment, Holliday's right hand was bent back awkwardly on his dive into Beltre's shoe, and the Cardinals cleanup hitter had to exit the game. His World Series was over.

As unfortunate as that might have been, what happened to Holliday on the night of August 22 truly epitomized his wild and crazy year. He was minding his own business, manning left field in the eighth inning of just another game in a pennant race when a giant moth flew into his right ear.

And stayed there.

Holliday tried to dislodge the bug for a couple of pitches, but when it wouldn't budge, he called timeout and trotted off the field. Several uncomfortable minutes would be needed to remove the bug. "As you can imagine, having something in your ear fluttering was not comfortable," Holliday said. "I started shaking my head like you do when you have water in your ear. I thought, *Well, that's not working.* I don't think I had my glove on for one pitch because I was trying to get it out. Then I was like, I can't handle this. That's when I called timeout."

How did he know what it was? "I knew it was a moth by the sound of the flutter," he deadpanned. Why Holliday? "Maybe I smell," he said. "Maybe I didn't put the bug spray on." How can you prevent something like that from happening again? "Wear some kind of ear muff," he said. "Maybe one in Cardinals' red. Let's get the Birds on the Bat put on there."

Holliday was able to joke the next day, but he wasn't laughing the previous night. Initial efforts to remove the moth called for Holliday to sit in a dark room so the moth might be attracted to the light leaking through the door and depart on its own. No luck. "It went in face first so it couldn't back out," Holliday said. "They don't have the ability to back out."

Holliday estimated the moth was in his ear for nearly 10 minutes after he departed the game before trainers finally removed it with the assistance of an otoscope and tweezers. The moth still was alive when it came out—but not for long. Holliday said he was not the killer. "So much wisdom passed onto him being inside my head that he died of an overflow of wisdom," Holliday said.

Matt Holliday readies himself to swing during 2011, a year in which he hit .296 with 22 home runs despite struggling through an appendicitis, a finger injury, and a weird insect malady.

With the deceased moth safely stored in a sandwich bag inside Holliday's locker the next day, he passed it around to show the media. Holliday was more annoyed than harmed by the untimely invasion and he also was a little concerned that the moth might have somehow reached his brain. The team doctor informed him that was not possible. "If it happens again, I won't panic," Holliday said.

He made sure the ear was cleaned out to prevent any further misfortune. "As long as they didn't lay babies while it was in there, I'll be okay," he said. "We washed it out with saline to make sure no larvae remained in there." In a season full of unusual misfortunes, Holliday listed this one as the strangest. "I don't get a lot of bugs in my ear," he said. As he stood in the clubhouse talking with reporters the next day, he was asked the inevitable question. Anything else bugging you?

* * *

Heading into the 2011 season, Holliday had been a .324 hitter in his time with the Cardinals. He had won a Silver Slugger award and been named to the National League All-Star team in 2010. Acquired a week before the trade deadline in 2009 to boost the offense for the pennant stretch, Holliday's impact was immediate and huge. He went 20-for-33 (.606) in his first nine games and within a month after the trade, the Cardinals had blown out a one-and-a-half-game lead in the NL Central to eight games.

Despite his exploits with the bat, Holliday had become best known to Cardinals fans for his defense—or lack thereof. The Cardinals enjoyed the NL's best record after Holliday arrived to end a two-year playoff drought. Their hopes were high as they went west to face the Los Angeles Dodgers in the National League Division Series. But they didn't win a game against the Dodgers, and Holliday's glove was a key reason why.

After Chris Carpenter was roughed up in a 5–3, Game 1 loss, the Cardinals needed a victory in Game 2 to stay out of a 2–0 hole in the best-of-five series. Adam Wainwright delivered an eight-inning gem, and a homer by Holliday had helped the Cardinals take a 2–1 lead into the ninth inning. The first two Dodgers made outs, and closer Ryan Franklin came within one strike from sending the series to St. Louis tied. Then, with the count to 2–2 on James Loney, Franklin unleashed a 93 mph fastball that the lefty-hitting Loney sliced to Holliday in left field for what appeared to be a routine fly that would end the game.

Holliday had to run to the ball, but he had it within his grasp in plenty of time. But he missed the ball. Instead of game over, the Dodgers had the tying run on second. Franklin was unable to regroup. He walked two and gave up two hits before the Dodgers walked off with a 3–2 victory. Suddenly the Cardinals were a loss from elimination, and Holliday was left explaining how he missed such a catchable fly. "I feel terrible, but I just missed the ball," he said to a swarm of media crowding him inside the visitors' clubhouse. "It hit my stomach. I think I can catch a ball hit right at me."

The series seemed over. The Cardinals had already used their aces and still were down 2–0. The big question became how would the fans welcome Holliday at Busch Stadium during player introductions before Game 3. He would become a free agent when the season ended, and the Cardinals had made their intentions clear that they wanted to sign him to a long-term deal. They had tried trading for him before the Colorado Rockies moved him to Oakland before the 2009 season. And now that they finally had him, they wanted him to stay. Holliday had enjoyed a strong second half, too, with a .353 batting average and 13 home runs in 63 games.

Like many before him, Holliday also had become enamored with playing in front of nightly crowds of 40,000 at Busch Stadium. As costly as the error in L.A. had been, few expected he would be booed by the forgiving faithful. Unlike Philadelphia fans and their reputation for being rude, Cardinals fans had the opposite rep of being appreciative and kind. Still, few could have expected him to receive a louder cheer than

Albert Pujols. But Holliday was given a long and loud standing ovation in pregame introductions, and another roar went up when he approached the batter's box for his first at-bat. It didn't matter that day, though, as the Cardinals bowed out quietly in a 5–1 loss. Holliday went 0-for-4 and finished the series without another hit beside his Game 2 homer.

Holliday kept the media waiting at his locker for nearly 45 minutes after the game before he addressed the series and, more importantly, his future. He was decidedly noncommittal about returning to St. Louis, though that might have been a negotiating ploy based on a conversation we had years later. "I had been excited to finally end up here. From the beginning it was everything I expected it would be and more," Holliday said. "So after the season, I sat down with [agent] Scott [Boras] and told him, 'Look, this is my first choice. If the offer is anywhere near in the same ballpark, this is where I want to be.'"

Though the negotiations took longer than Holliday and the Cardinals anticipated, in early January of 2010, he agreed to a seven-year, $120 million deal that remains the largest in the history of the franchise. Holliday announced then that the Cardinals would be getting more than a ballplayer. The Hollidays would make St. Louis their home 12 months a year.

The deal has worked out about as well as possible for both the Hollidays and the Cardinals. Holliday helped the Cardinals make the playoffs every year except 2010 and has been one of the National League's top three offensive forces. He has become an active member of the community, and St. Louis has become the only home that his four children really have known.

Though his personality is reserved and he avoids talking about himself nearly every chance he can, Holliday has become a leader of the franchise. He is the oldest member of the lineup and sets the example for work ethic. He even brings in the organization's prospects for offseason workouts on his own dime. The ping-pong table that sits in the middle of the clubhouse also was his idea.

Manager Mike Matheny calls him a "freak" for how hard he hits a baseball. Teammate Adam Wainwright calls him a "monster" in the weight room. A clubhouse full of teammates talk about what a good teammate he is. His general manager only can wish that every acquisition proved to be so successful. "It's been a win-win," John Mozeliak said. "He's been an elite player who's helped us win a world championship and reach two World Series. As a person he's done a lot for our community. To see what he and his family mean to St. Louis means a lot. It's worked out tremendously."

For those who watched him grow up in Oklahoma, his success hardly is a surprise. Matt Holliday always has been the stud athlete. The son of a coach and from a family of elite athletes, he grew up at ball fields. As a kid, Matt was the best in whatever league he joined in Stillwater, Oklahoma, and usually there was no close second. He hit the baseball so hard the other parents requested he be moved to a higher level because they were concerned with the safety of their sons. "He nearly decapitated a couple of pitchers, and they decided he needed to move up," said his mom, Kathy Holliday. "They thought he was dangerous. From the time he was little, he always hit the ball really hard up the middle."

Matt made the varsity baseball team as a ninth-grader when he already stood a hearty 6'3". As a senior he had to decide whether to play baseball and football in college or focus on baseball and be paid an $842,500 signing bonus. Few who saw him at Stillwater High doubted he could have played quarterback in the NFL, but baseball proved to be his calling. "When he was about eight years old, he told me he was going to be a professional baseball player," Kathy said. "I said, 'That's great, but you need to have a backup plan. Everybody needs a backup plan.' He said, 'Well, fine, then, I'll be a professional football player.' That's not what I was thinking, but he stuck to it."

Matt paid his dues for six years in the minor leagues before an out-field spot opened in Colorado. Once promoted to the Rockies—his big league debut came at Busch Stadium in 2004—he never was sent down. He made the All-Star team for the first time in his second full season, and by the time he led the Rockies to the 2007 World Series, there was little doubt he would score a superstar contract when he became a free agent.

The Rockies didn't believe they could re-sign him long term so they shopped him before the 2009 season. Though the Cardinals were among the final teams in consideration, the Rockies shipped Matt to Oakland. Three months later, however, with the A's in last place, the Cardinals got their man.

Pujols Beats the Odds

When Albert Pujols still was El Hombre in St. Louis, you could open the main doors to the Cardinals clubhouse, and his locker stood straight ahead on the far wall. Yadier Molina's was to his right, and Lance Berkman's was to his left. Like most players when their team is at home, Pujols seldom was sitting at his stall when the media was granted access to the clubhouse. But on June 23, 2011, four days after he had broken a bone in his left arm, he had no place else to be a few hours before that night's game against the Philadelphia Phillies. After all, he did not need to work in the batting cage or study in the video room.

Approaching Albert at his locker wasn't always the most comfortable feeling. If he didn't feel like talking—and that was often the case—he sometimes wasn't exactly polite in sending you on your way. He had more important duties than filling up our notebooks. But I had just one question and thought it was a pretty easy one. "Albert, if you make the All-Star team, will you go to Phoenix, even though you won't be able to play?"

Pujols had made the All-Star team in nine of his 10 seasons, missing out only in his second year (even though he had 21 homers and 66 RBIs by the break). Whether he said yes or no about this one, his answer would be newsworthy. By the cold look that Pujols gave me, I could tell he did not like the question. Perhaps he was offended because I had said "if" instead of "when" about making the All-Star team. He was hitting an uncharacteristic .279 but still ranked among league leaders with 17 homers. And he was Albert Pujols, one of the biggest names in the game. But Pujols wasn't worried about making or not making the All-Star Game. He wasn't thinking that far ahead. "Who says I won't be back by the All-Star break?" He asked.

I chuckled. He had to be kidding. Two days earlier, the Cardinals had announced he would be out until August. He was dealing with a broken bone—not a tweaked ankle. And he's talking about returning in two weeks? Come on. But Pujols didn't kid around much, especially not about his playing time. "You're supposed to be out for at least a month," I reminded him.

He shook his head. "Who knows," he said.

To become the only player in major league history to begin their career with 10 consecutive seasons of hitting .300 with 30 homers and 100 RBIs required more than talent and hard work. An ability to produce when less than completely healthy was almost as important. As amazing as Pujols was with his bat, his ability to play through pain might have been his greatest asset in St. Louis. The season before he moved to first base, he played with his right elbow such a mess that Tony La Russa ordered him to not throw the ball, a difficult proposition for a left fielder. But La Russa could trust Pujols to lob the ball in from left field. If that's what he had to do to stay in the lineup, no problem.

For years Pujols treaded gingerly through the clubhouse because of plantar fasciitis. He dealt with sore knees, strained shoulders, and ailing legs. I have little doubt that his production slipped faster than expected in Anaheim because of the beating he absorbed in St. Louis. He showed an amazing ability to come back from injuries throughout his 11 years with the Cardinals. Pujols landed on the disabled list three times in St.

Louis, and each time he was expected to miss considerably more than the 15-day minimum. He never took more than 17 days to return.

This gift for healing never was exhibited any better than after the injury he suffered on that Sunday afternoon at Busch Stadium. Pujols just had broken a 2–2 tie against the Kansas City Royals by slugging his 17th home run in the bottom of the fifth inning when he returned to first base for the top of the sixth.

Kansas City's first batter, Wilson Betemit, hit a grounder up the middle that Pete Kozma, a shortstop then playing second base, ranged up the middle and fielded. He jumped, spun, and fired to first, but his throw sailed well to the home-plate side of the base. Pujols stretched out with his glove arm extended to make the catch as Betemit, smelling a hit, hustled toward first. Just as ball reached glove, Betemit ran into Pujols' outstretched arm, and the first baseman's left wrist snapped awkwardly. His glove went flying, and Pujols' pain was obvious. He hopped off the field, jumped a couple of times, and crumbled to the ground with his right hand holding his left.

X-Rays confirmed what the Cardinals feared: a broken bone. Pujols had suffered a non-displaced fracture in his left forearm and would stay in a cast for three weeks. The Cardinals said they would be without their slugger for between four and six weeks. Two days later Pujols showed off his cast and admitted having regrets over how he played the ball. "You wish you could go back two days and if you knew that was coming, let [the ball] go or something," he said. "That's not the way I play the game."

Asked if he would need a full six weeks before he could return, he turned testy. "I am a ballplayer. I don't know anything about medicine," he said. "I need to listen to them. Whatever they tell me to do to recover, that's it. The one thing that I don't want to do is try and rush it. We still have three months in the season left. To rush back and make it worse and then have it bother me the rest of the season, I don't want to do that."

Less than a week later, a Cardinals official told me they had overheard

Pujols earlier that day talking on the phone in the reception area of the home team's clubhouse. Albert was smiling and chatting hurriedly. "I don't know who he was talking to, but he said he's been lifting weights and he's already started to swing the bat," the employee told me. "He was talking like he will be back well before a month."

Pujols had started taking swings barely a week after suffering the injury. He ended up missing only 17 days, beating the team's initial time-table by at least 13 days. He was back in time to play five games before the All-Star break, collecting only one hit in the first three but then five in the next two. He did not attend the All-Star Game because he wasn't selected to the team for the first time since 2002. That was a mistake by National League manager Bruce Bochy, but time off at the All-Star break would benefit Pujols and his wrist far more than a couple of days in the desert. Pujols had served as unofficial host for the 2009 All-Star Game at Busch Stadium and was so busy appearing here and there that he needed a break after the break. He did not mind having the down time for once.

Pujols came back in the second half and carried the Cardinals through their late-season charge to the pennant. He hit .319 with 19 homers and 49 RBIs after the break. No other Cardinal had more than nine homers or 34 RBIs in the second half.

Rasmus Moves On

On a Sunday morning in September 2010, Colby Rasmus sat by himself at a table in the southeast corner of the Cardinals clubhouse. Though this season would be the best of his six-year career, he wasn't the happiest camper. His problems with Tony La Russa had become a hot topic in St. Louis, and on this day, his manager had confirmed to the *St. Louis Post-Dispatch* that Rasmus had requested a trade.

When a small group of reporters approached Rasmus for the details, he appeared more confused than disgruntled. He said he had not asked to be dealt, though perhaps he was referring to that weekend. The request had been made in late July, following a closed-door meeting. He denied telling general manager John Mozeliak he wanted out, but he also made it clear that he wasn't thrilled to be in St. Louis.

Do you like it here?

"I'd rather not answer that if I don't have to," he said.

Do you want to be here next year?

"I'm not going to say either way. I'm going to come in and play hard every day."

Now you know those answers will be interpreted as "no, you don't want to be here."

"I didn't say that, though," Rasmus replied.

So are you saying you don't know?

"I'd like to be here, but there's no telling," he said. "I'd rather say nothing so you won't write nothing, if you don't mind. But you do what you want."

I left the clubhouse that day believing that Colby Rasmus' days wearing the Birds on the Bat were numbered. He was not traded that season or even during the offseason. The Cardinals weren't ready to give up on the 24-year-old who had been their most ballyhooed prospect practically since they drafted him in the first round out of an Alabama high school in 2005.

Whatever trouble he might have had getting along with his manager and teammates, he still had hit 23 homers, scored 85 runs, and put up an .859 on-base-plus slugging percentage (OPS) that was the best among National League center fielders in 2010. Those numbers compared favorably to another 24-year-old center fielder, Andrew McCutchen.

If Mozeliak had not decided to reboot the club's pitching staff shortly before the July 31, 2011, trade deadline, Rasmus might have continued to roam center field in St. Louis. The GM admitted he could have received a better return on Rasmus by moving him the previous winter.

By the time the Cardinals made the move four days before the trade deadline, Rasmus had been relegated to backup duty, playing behind Jon Jay. Rasmus' production had slipped in every month with a batting average of .182 in July. Still, he was only 24 and possessed an abundance of power and speed and already had enjoyed two solid seasons in the majors.

The three-team deal that sent Rasmus and three relievers to the Toronto Blue Jays brought the Cardinals a durable starter in Edwin Jackson, a well-traveled right-handed reliever in Octavio Dotel, and a capable lefty in Marc Rzepczynski. With Jay playing well and the Cardinals in need of a pitching boost, the trade looked like one that would help the Cardinals and the Blue Jays. "This is a window to win," Mozeliak said at a news conference to announce the deal. "Today we feel like we're a better team than we were yesterday."

"It's probably best for both parties that Colby gets a fresh start," Blue Jays general manager Alex Anthopoulos told reporters. "I think he's going to fit in great and he's going to thrive."

Most of the national experts scored the deal a big victory for the Blue Jays. They screamed, how could the Cardinals give up on such a promising young player? Wrote Keith Law for ESPN, echoing the sentiments of many: "The Cardinals have made a terrible organizational move by allowing their aging manager to run off the best hitting prospect the team has produced since drafting Albert Pujols." Said Jim Bowden, an ex-general manager also working for ESPN: "This deal will come back to haunt them and sooner than they think. The Cardinals better win this year or they will really regret this one. Worst trade of the year, sorry Cardinals fans."

(Not to pat myself on the back or anything, but as a St. Louis-based baseball writer for *The Sporting News* at the time, I had spent enough time around Rasmus to offer a more tempered analysis. I wrote, "The No. 1 message to take away from the Colby Rasmus trade: the St. Louis Cardinals are going for it now. They need pitching and they are getting three pitchers who will improve a rotation and bullpen that have been suspect in recent weeks.")

More than three and a half years later, plenty of time for hindsight, calling the deal "terrible" for the Cardinals would be a mistake. Still trying to live up to his prospect billing, Rasmus hit .225 in 2014 and lost his starting job. Jay has had his ups and downs, but after a strong 2014, he was set to enter 2015 as the Cardinals' center fielder. Rasmus has hit more homers (66–17), but Jay owns the edge in other notable numbers. Jay has hit .291/.359/.385 with a .743 OPS, 223 runs, 288 strikeouts, and 124 walks since Rasmus departed. Rasmus went .234/.295/.433 with a .728 OPS, 191 runs, 447 strikeouts, and 118 walks with the Blue Jays.

The Cardinals weren't finished wheeling and dealing. Four days after moving Rasmus, they sent a prospect to the Los Angeles Dodgers for veteran shortstop Rafael Furcal. Though he had been limited by injuries much of the season, Furcal had regained his health and had started hitting. He filled two needs for the Cardinals, providing a much-needed upgrade on defense and giving them a prototypical leadoff hitter.

He also brought a loud presence to the clubhouse. Along with the addition of Dotel, the noise level was cranked up in what had been a fairly quiet clubhouse. "When I came here I found a team that was kind of quiet," Furcal later told the *Los Angeles Times*. "I'm not the kind of guy who plays baseball quietly. I like to talk, joke, and keep everyone happy. That's how baseball should be. You should leave the field *happy*."

Before long, Furcal introduced the term to his new teammates, and they would repeat it through the end of the season. "Happy flight," would ring through the clubhouse every time they won the final game of a series before hopping on a plane. With the roster sufficiently beefed up, the Cardinals would enjoy many happy flights over the next three months.

The Cards' Clutch Carpenter

More often than not, "players only" team meetings are overrated. Media and fans like to hear about them, but unless a specific issue needs to be hashed out, gathering the guys and having a couple of veterans stand up and say the team must play better doesn't often make much of a difference in the standings.

But every now and then, a player comes along who truly can impact the course of the club with a few chosen words delivered at the right time. Chris Carpenter was one of those players. He not only epitomized professionalism during nine years with the Cardinals and commanded as much respect from his teammates as any player, but he also stands 6'6" and looked about nine feet tall when standing on the mound. Just from the sight of him, you could tell that Chris Carpenter was one of those guys who you better listen to.

Anyone who witnessed the Cardinals-Reds brawl in 2010 also can attest to Carpenter's concern for his teammates and his passion toward the game. He wore Johnny Cueto's spike marks on his back for weeks after he stepped in the middle of the benches-clearing blowup and was pushed to the backstop at Great American Ball Park, where Cincinnati's Cueto was flailing with his feet. "We had some guy kicking me in the back, who ends up kicking my backup catcher [Jason LaRue] and splits his face open," Carpenter said. "When you see him, you'll see he could have done some real damage. He got him in the side of the eye, his nose, his face. Totally unprofessional. Unbelievable. I haven't seen anything like that."

Carpenter never was accused of cheap-shotting an opponent, but he developed a reputation for rankling them, especially in the National League Central. If a batter had the nerve to question the umpire after a called third strike from Carpenter, he could count on a glare following him back to the dugout. His fire too much to hold in at times, Carpenter screamed after big outs and shouted into his glove after frustrating plays. Some opponents made no secret of what they thought about the big right-hander. "No one really likes Carpenter," said then Brewers pitcher Zack Greinke during the 2011 National League Championship Series. "They think his presence, his attitude out there sometimes is phony. He yells at people. He just stares people down and stuff. Most pitchers just don't do that."

Carpenter's tirades weren't limited to opponents, though, as Brendan Ryan can attest. When he was late arriving at his shortstop position one inning when Carpenter was pitching, Ryan's days in St. Louis soon became numbered, and he was traded in the offseason. Carpenter was as invested in the Cardinals as the club was in him and he would do anything within his power to help them succeed.

At some point when the Cardinals were being swept by the Los Angeles Dodgers in a three-game series that ended on August 24, 2011, Carpenter and a few other veterans decided a players-only meeting was needed. The team had stumbled to a 10–12 record since the trade deadline and fallen a seemingly hopeless 10½ games out in the wild-card race.

Carpenter was not out to deliver any phony pep talk about how the team could rally and make the playoffs. His message was more tangible. He wanted to make sure that everyone in the clubhouse continued to put forth a professional effort, regardless of the deficit in the standings. The fans were owed that much, he told his teammates. "Everybody understood where we were at and what was going on," Carpenter later said. "Even if we don't win another game the rest of the year, we were going to go out and make an effort and at least show people that we're going to make that effort and not embarrass ourselves. Did it help? I don't know." He added, "I know we started playing better after that."

A lot better.

Five weeks after the players-only meeting, on the final day of the regular season, Carpenter pitched a two-hit shutout at Houston that completed a 23–9 season-ending run for the Cardinals and wiped out the last of their 10½-game deficit. Two hours later, when the Philadelphia

Phillies beat the Atlanta Braves 4–3 in 13 innings, the Cardinals had clinched a spot in the playoffs.

They were just getting started.

* * *

It was 1–0 Cardinals in the bottom of the ninth of the decisive game in the National League Division Series against the 102-win Philadelphia Phillies. Carpenter, nothing short of brilliant all night, had one out to go when manager Tony La Russa surveyed the scene and saw his ace… smiling. Yes, the man notorious for his scowl had let down his guard. Blink and you might have missed it. Perhaps Carpenter was reflecting on how far the Cardinals had come since the players-only meeting he had called in August. Seemingly out of the playoff race then, the Cardinals were one out from advancing to the NLCS for the first time since 2006. Or maybe Carpenter, 36 at the time, was reflecting on the end of a three-year stretch during which he had not endured any disabling shoulder inflammation, elbow problems, or mysterious nerve issues in his right arm. Carpenter had arrived in the majors 14 years earlier, but this was the first time he had made it through three consecutive seasons without an arm injury putting him on the sideline.

Or Carpenter could have been thinking about how close he was to beating his good friend and former teammate in Toronto, Roy Halladay. This was the first time they had started against each other, and they had delivered a duel befitting Cy Young Award winners. Both were at the top of their game. The Cardinals had scored the game's only run in the first inning when leadoff hitter Rafael Furcal tripled off Halladay and scored when the next batter, Skip Schumaker, doubled to right field after he had fouled off five two-strike pitches.

Halladay had allowed only three Cardinals to reach base over the next six innings. In the eighth he loaded the bases with one out but quelled the threat when he struck out Lance Berkman and retired Matt Holliday on a fly to left. Carpenter had been in control all night, scattering three hits and allowing only one runner to third base. The closest the Phillies had come to scoring was when Chase Utley flew out to deep center field for the first out in the bottom of the ninth inning. Hunter Pence grounded out to third for the second out. As Carpenter prepared to get the last out, against cleanup hitter Ryan Howard, La Russa saw his ace with that uncharacteristic grin.

Howard, a native St. Louisan, had scared the Cardinals in his previous at-bat when, swinging on a 3–0 count, he hit a line drive to right field that Lance Berkman tracked down. This time, with the Phillies just one swing from tying the game, Howard grounded to second on a 2–2 curveball. He barely made his way out of the batter's box before he crumbled to the ground. His left Achilles had obliterated, and the Phillies' season had gone kaput.

The Cardinals, meanwhile, stormed Carpenter, and another celebration was on. As the partying went on inside the visitors' clubhouse, La Russa came upon the winning pitcher and asked him about that smile. La Russa recounted Carpenter's reply in his book, *One Last Strike.* "What else was I supposed to do," Carpenter said. "I was having fun out there."

Even more fun was ahead.

Often overlooked about the Cardinals' run to the championship in 2011 was the weather. Specifically, rain forced a one-day postponement of Game 6 of the World Series. Instead of playing on a Wednesday following a travel day on Tuesday, Game 6 was pushed to Thursday. The delay left the Rangers with more idle time in a strange town to think about their 3–2 lead. The extra day proved even more significant to the Cardinals.

Now if a Game 7 was needed, Chris Carpenter would be able to start. After pitching seven innings in the Cardinals' 4–2 Game 5 loss on Monday night, Carpenter still would be working on three instead of the typical four days rest if the Series went to a Game 7. But without a postponement, no way he would have started Game 7. Only once in his career had Carpenter started on short rest, and that was between the regular season and the NLDS opener against the Phillies. He lasted only three innings and gave up four runs.

After David Freese sent the series to a seventh game with his walk-off homer in Game 6, La Russa played coy in his news conference and did not name his starter for the next night. "Might just roll Jake back out there, who knows," La Russa said, referring to Jake Westbrook, the veteran sinkerballer who had just picked up the win in Game 6 with a scoreless inning of relief.

Anyone who was paying attention believed Carpenter would get the call for the final game. His short-rest start against the Phillies had been his only poor outing of the playoffs. He had pitched well in his Game 3 start of the NLCS and had won Game 1 of the World Series with six solid innings. He had pitched even better—two runs in seven innings—in Game 5 at Rangers Ballpark, but the Rangers scored twice in the eighth to win 4–2 and move within one victory of their first World Series title. During that start, TV cameras had caught Carpenter at his fieriest.

After Rangers catcher Mike Napoli, who already had homered off Carpenter in Game 1, flew out to deep center field for the last out in the sixth inning, he was minding his own business when cameras caught the Cardinals starter unleashing a few choice words in his direction. It didn't take much of a lip reader to see they were R-rated. "Fuck yeah! You piece of shit! Fuck you!" Carpenter screamed.

Napoli, understandably, seemed confused and after the game told reporters he had no idea what had happened. The two had no history, and Napoli had said absolutely nothing to the Cardinals starter. This was just Carpenter being Carpenter. Back at Busch Stadium the next day, he talked as though he did not know his tirade had been caught on camera. "Did somebody say something about me yelling at somebody?" Carpenter asked.

It would not have been the first time Carpenter used the "I was too locked in to know what I was doing" explanation. His teammates admitted they sometimes couldn't tell if he was yelling at himself or an opponent. Asked if he had been talking to himself this time, Carpenter said only, "Stuff happens."

* * *

Though no one was remotely aware at the time, when Chris Carpenter left Game 7 with a 5–2 lead after six innings, he would be walking off the Busch Stadium mound with a win for the last time. His right arm would not be at full strength again. Carpenter would pitch, or try to pitch, for two more years, but he won only one more game—in the NLDS at Washington in 2012.

His career did not end without a fight—or two or three. When Carpenter reported to spring training in 2012, he was penciled in as the Opening Day starter and he said he felt fit. "I'm excited about where I'm at," he said one morning in February inside the clubhouse at Roger Dean Stadium. "I'm not concerned about my body."

Carpenter believed a new weightlifting program that focused on lifting slightly heavier weights had made his right shoulder stronger than the year before. He was able to begin his throwing program without incident in January, the same time he started in the offseasons when the Cardinals hadn't won the World Series. But his shoulder soon started giving out on him. He did not make a start in spring training, began the season on the disabled list, and had given up on pitching in 2012 by June.

In July he underwent a complex surgery to relieve thoracic outlet syndrome during which a rib on his right side was removed to relieve pressure on the nerves that stretched from his shoulder area to his neck. Doctors said that, barring setbacks, Carpenter should be ready for spring training in 2013.

Remarkably, he returned even sooner. Barely two months after undergoing the procedure, Carpenter started against the Chicago Cubs at Wrigley Field. His fastball barely touched 90 mph, but he went five innings and allowed two runs. He made two more starts in the regular season and then three in the postseason, relying far more on his savvy than his stuff.

Carpenter went into the offseason much like the year before, believing he would be 100 percent for 2013. He even started his throwing program earlier than usual and was all set to report to Jupiter, Florida. But two weeks before pitchers and catchers reported to spring training, Carpenter shut down his throwing indefinitely. As he had increased the intensity of his pitching in his informal bullpen sessions, the pain in his right arm also increased. The nerve issue that had led to surgery in 2012 had returned. In the week before he stopped throwing, his right hand even turned "red then purple...that's probably not a good thing," he said, believing he had a circulation problem.

"I'm sick and tired of dealing with arm stuff," he said at a February 11 press conference at Busch Stadium. "I was feeling good this winter. I was excited about this year and looking forward to pitch. Right now, that's not going to happen." Carpenter admitted plenty of tears had been shed in sadness as well as frustration. For days after he had told general manager John Mozeliak that he no longer could throw, he still had not returned the many calls and messages from his teammates. Carpenter said he would not be heading to Florida for spring training in part to avoid being a distraction. He also did not want to spend any more time around the team without feeling like a part of it.

But Carpenter still held hope that he could pitch again. He continued to work out just as he normally would, doing everything but picking up a baseball. He said he would do whatever he could to return except undergo another surgery. Eight was enough, he said.

By May, after several sessions of playing catch with his then 10-year-old son in the backyard, the life in his right arm began to return. He slowly tried another comeback and even made two rehab starts in the minor leagues. To the casual observer, he looked like he was on his way. But after he gave up nine hits and four runs while getting only 10 outs in his second rehab start, he shut himself down again. "We're going to back off and try to figure out what's going on," said Carpenter, still not ready to give up. "I'm going to make sure I'm still doing the right things and moving in the right direction. We're going to back off and see what happens."

A month later, Carpenter had come to terms with his baseball future. His right arm was not going to cooperate. His pitching days were finished. His latest comeback attempt had not ended the way he wanted, but by trying that last time, Carpenter found peace of mind. "Answering the question for myself about not coming back is what allowed me to get over that frustration and disappointment," Carpenter told me in late August of 2013.

But he still was under contract and, though he had stayed away from his teammates for much of the season, he finally accepted an invitation from manager Mike Matheny to join the fellows for the final weeks. Carpenter took grounders during batting practice, played cheerleader in the dugout, and went on road trips with the club. "If this is the last time I'm going to be part of a team, I want to put this uniform on, go out there, and enjoy the major league baseball atmosphere and experience," he said.

Carpenter stayed with the Cardinals through their postseason run to the World Series, and the club announced his retirement in November. Carpenter has yet to hold a formal news conference, though he made himself available to a few reporters and me when he visited spring training in 2014. Of the 11 seasons he spent under contract with the Cardinals, Carpenter missed virtually five seasons. But in the six seasons when he was healthy, he became one of the best pitchers in franchise history. He won 95 games and lost only 44 to go with a 3.07 ERA. He won a franchise-record 10 games in the postseason. He also won the 2005 NL Cy Young Award and—not one, but—two NL Comeback Player of the Year awards.

Carpenter's impact stretched beyond statistics and team meetings, too. He started the ritual of having the team's starting pitchers watch each other's side sessions, a practice that has spread to other teams. He lockered beside and worked closely with Lance Lynn to harness his emotions and he served as mentor to Adam Wainwright, among others.

During 2014, Carpenter visited for the first time as a non-player. He had been hired for an undefined role the club hoped would evolve. The club simply wanted him around, and he wanted to be around. On one of his first days in camp, shortly after the players boarded a bus for an exhibition against the Mets, Carpenter hopped behind the wheel of an oversized SUV to chauffeur Mozeliak and other front-office members to Port St. Lucie. After all his years of leading the Cardinals' rotation, Carpenter had found another way to drive the team.

Legend of the Rally Squirrel

When a fan in Philadelphia threw a stuffed squirrel into the visitors' bullpen during the Chris Carpenter-Roy Halladay Game 5 duel, he was just trying to be cute. Why not poke fun at the Cardinals? Earlier that week at Busch Stadium, an actual squirrel had appeared on the field during Game 3 of the National League Division Series, and again in Game 4, a squirrel scampered right across the plate when Skip Schumaker was batting. When the Cardinals scored twice in the next inning to break a 3–3 tie and went on to a 5–3 victory that forced Game 5, a star was born.

The Rally Squirrel soon had a Twitter account, was appearing on T-shirts, and starring in commercials. Who could blame Philly fans for teasing the Cardinals about the nutty antics? But the Cardinals would have the last laugh. Reliever Octavio Dotel scooped up the stuffed critter and proclaimed it a good luck charm. After the 1–0 victory, he decided to tote it around as long as the Cardinals kept playing. The Rally Squirrel ended up getting doused with champagne in celebrations following Game 5, the National League Championship Series, and the World Series. The Cardinals trotted out a squirrel mascot to keep Fredbird company during the World Series, and a tiny depiction of a squirrel even made it onto the Cardinals' championship rings.

Perhaps in the superstitious world of baseball, the Rally Squirrel brought the Cardinals some good fortune. Dotel served as its primary caretaker and he enjoyed the best month of his career. The 13-year veteran on his 12th team won the first and only World Series of his career. He played a key role, too.

The St. Louis bullpen, in fact, proved the difference in the Cardinals' six-game victory over the Milwaukee Brewers in the NLCS. Cardinals relievers pitched more innings than their starters in the series and with much better results. The bullpen went 3–0 with a 1.88 ERA in 28⅔ innings while the starters went 1–2 with a 7.03 ERA in 24⅓ innings.

The deadline deals to bolster the bullpen had paid off. The Cardinals wanted Dotel for his versatility and ability to bounce back quickly after outings and he delivered on both counts. The well-traveled veteran pitched in five of his first six games with the Cardinals after being traded. Before the end of the regular season, he had been called on by Tony La Russa to pitch in every inning from the fourth to the 11th.

Most relievers prefer to know when they are likely to be called so they can establish a routine during the game. Dotel typically had watched the first three innings of a game in the clubhouse before heading to the bullpen, where he would start to loosen when he sensed a situation was coming that might call for him. With the Cardinals, he had to change his thinking. He had no idea when his number would be called and he wasn't alone. Through the NLCS and World Series, La

Russa sometimes was ringing for relievers before the crowd had settled in. Routines became anything except routine. "You would love to know what inning you are going to come in but with Tony, you don't know," Dotel said. "It's tough, I'm not going to lie."

But the uncertainty also provided Dotel an edge that proved helpful in the pressure-packed playoffs. "It's good you don't know because you have to be ready mentally and prepare for any inning, any time, any moment," he said. In the NLCS Dotel's main role was to face Brewers slugger Ryan Braun, who was as hot as any hitter that postseason. Braun entered the NLCS after going 9-for-18 in the NLDS. He also entered having gone 2-for-8 against Dotel in his career with all six outs coming via strikeouts.

There may have been no bigger at-bat for Milwaukee in the entire NLCS than when Braun stepped up in the fifth inning of Game 5. The series was tied, and the Cardinals led 4–1, but the Brewers were rallying. They had a run in, two on, and their best hitter coming up. And Dotel was coming in. After throwing five straight fastballs, Dotel got Braun to whiff on a 2–2 slider that ended what would be the Brewers' last scoring threat. "I will be honest. I feel like I save the game right there," Dotel said. "Two guys on base and I'm facing Mr. Braun. The game can change right there."

The next night in the Cardinals' clincher, Dotel struck out Braun again—this time on three pitches. "Just lucky," Dotel said. Maybe so. He was clutching the Rally Squirrel, wet from a champagne spraying, as he talked.

Motte's Moxie on the Mound and Off

Just as the Cardinals' playoff hopes were soaring, they came crashing down on the afternoon of September 22 at Busch Stadium. They led the Mets 6–2 in the top of the ninth and were just three outs from cutting what had been a 10½-game deficit on August 22 to a single game.

Not taking any chances, Tony La Russa sent out his new but yet-to-be-anointed closer, Jason Motte, to secure the win, even though it wasn't a save situation. A key to the Cardinals' late-season charge had been solidifying the bullpen and a key to the pen had been Motte.

He was the only reliever who had been up with the Cardinals all season, and his role had evolved from undefined to set-up situations to the ninth inning. He did not allow an earned run from late June through early September and converted eight of nine chances during the team's 19–6 stretch that had put them back in contention. He did not allow a run in July or August and had given up only one in the first half of September. But he had been working a lot—15 times in the 25 games leading into that Thursday afternoon.

In need of only three outs and with a four-run lead to protect, this looked like Motte's easiest assignment in weeks. Even after he walked Willie Harris to lead off the ninth, no one seemed alarmed when Motte came back and induced a ground ball from Nick Evans, the next batter, that looked like a routine double play. But sure-handed shortstop Rafael Furcal didn't field the ball cleanly, and both runners were safe. Instead of two out with nobody on, Motte was facing two on with nobody out.

When Josh Thole flew out, the game could have been—and should have been—over. But it was far from it. Motte walked Jason Pridie on five pitches to load the bases and bring the tying run to the plate. Justin Turner did not get a hit, but he changed the game when he fouled off four two-strike pitches and worked a walk to cut the Cardinals' lead to 6–3.

Motte's day was done, but the Mets were not. Lefty Marc Rzepczynski was called in to face switch-hitter Jose Reyes and gave up a run-scoring single to make the score 6–4. La Russa then called on Fernando Salas, who worked ahead of Ruben Tejada before giving up a two-run double that tied the game and left the Mets with runners on second and third and still only one out.

Salas intentionally walked Angel Pagan and struck out David Wright for the second out. Salas then got two strikes on Harris before giving up a two-run single to right. The Mets led 8–6, and when the Cardinals went down 1-2-3 in their half of the ninth, the large afternoon crowd was stunned, and the home clubhouse was silenced. The playoffs that had seemed within reach just an inning earlier now seemed as far away as ever. Teams don't make up two-game deficits in six games very often. "I felt fine going out there. The ball was just kind of moving all over the place," said Motte, refusing to blame a heavy workload. "One would sink, one would run, one would cut. I was doing everything I could. It just wasn't going really anywhere I wanted it to go."

La Russa admitted fatigue could have been a factor, but the manager strongly defended his decision to go with Motte. "We have a four-run lead and we want to close out the win. You don't want to take any chance. I thought he was a better shot than having to push Salas, who could have used two days off." The skipper also defended his reasoning for having refused to designate Motte as his closer during the Cardinals' September surge. "He may be getting distracted by somebody thinking he's the closer," La Russa said in his postgame presser. "He should keep his focus on, just pitch as good as he can. He's not the closer. He's the closer a lot of times. He doesn't need to be distracted with that nonsense. He's not the closer for next year. That's just not in his best interest or ours to distract guys."

La Russa refused to call Motte his closer over the next five weeks, even though no one else saved a game for the Cardinals through the end of the World Series. Motte went 5-for-5 in save chances during the postseason, though he was the loser in Game 2 of the World Series when he entered in the ninth with a 1–0 lead and was charged with two runs. In the clubhouse after that game, Motte acted like a closer when he looked a large contingent of media at his locker and took responsibility for the 2–1 loss. "My job was to get them out and I didn't do it," said Motte, who faced two batters and gave up two hits. Both would score on sacrifice flies following a costly error by Albert Pujols.

Even though the first hit was a bloop single off the end of Ian Kinsler's bat, Motte didn't turn to bad luck as an excuse, even though La Russa said it would not usually result in a hit. "It doesn't matter," Motte said. "When you come in the ninth inning, you have a good day when your team wins. You can be up by three runs and let two runs in, have bases loaded, and get a pop-up to the warning track and guess what? You did your job. Or you can come in a one-run ballgame like [Game 2] and make some good pitches. They weren't good enough."

How long would the loss weigh on him? "Til you guys leave," Motte said, with a hint of a smile. Eight days later, after he was called on to protect another 6–2 lead—in Game 7 of the World Series—Motte was beaming from the bottom of a dog pile. Though he still didn't have the official designation, Motte was the closer for the World Series champions.

* * *

The thing that always has most impressed about Motte isn't his fastball, which he regularly cranked up to 100 mph before Tommy John surgery. Nor is it his Grizzly Adams beard, which he has kept since shortly after reaching the big leagues in 2008. (He says his wife, Caitlin, never has seen him clean-shaven.) It's not how he reached the majors just two years after converting from light-hitting catcher in the minors, even though he had not pitched since Little League. It wasn't even how he has addressed me as "sir" in many of our interviews.

No, it is his perspective. Jason Louis Motte gets it. He looks at life and his job the way every professional athlete should. He appreciates the talent he has been given and he understands the ability to throw a baseball 100 mph does not make him better than everyone else. Motte has always been as humble as anyone in the Cardinals' clubhouse, the kind of guy who takes the ball whenever he is asked and never has been concerned about his role. But he became far more than a good teammate when he sat out 2013 after undergoing season-ending surgery before he pitched in a single game. He became a hero.

With a smile on his face, time on his hands, and a huge assist from Caitlin, Motte made St. Louis and the entire major leagues a better place. Most players say that sitting out with injury is as difficult as their job gets because of the uncertainty and loneliness that follows. Motte did not have time for such feelings because he was too busy helping others. Whether he was cheering up young patients at area hospitals, promoting T-shirts for his Strike Out Cancer cause, or making appearances on behalf of his foundation, Motte thrived away from baseball. He said he didn't even miss being able to pitch for the Cardinals. "That sounds weird, but there was so much stuff I was able to do that I never would have gotten to do if I was playing," he said. "I wouldn't trade one out for all the people I got to meet and the stuff I got to do."

Now don't think Motte abandoned his day job for his charity work. He rehabbed daily after undergoing Tommy John surgery. "I worked my butt off," he said. "If you don't use your ability or try to use your ability to the best, than you're just wasting what God gave you."

He provided such a positive presence and inspiration at Busch Stadium that his teammates voted him the 2013 winner of the Darryl Kile Award, the first time an injured Cardinal was so honored. The award recognizes the player who exemplifies Kile's characteristics as "a good teammate, a great friend, a fine father, and a humble man." "The stuff I was able to do transcends baseball," Motte said. "Baseball put me in position to do some of these things, but baseball will be over at some point."

From the moment he felt his right elbow wasn't right early in spring training 2013 through his surgery, rehab, and his uneven comeback in 2014, Motte stayed focused on what he could do and not what he couldn't. "I looked at him one day and said, 'You're a far better person than me because I would not be accepting that this happened,'" Caitlin said. "He still has this great attitude and sense of peace that has been in his heart since this happened. He always says it's going to be okay, and we'll get through this."

As often happens, Motte found he could help himself by reaching out to others. "You see these kids with cancer going through a tough time, and they're fighting with a smile on their face," Motte said. "If they can do that, I sure can go through what I was going through. They have such a great outlook, taking one day at a time, and enjoying what you have on that day. Tomorrow may be a tough day, but you know what? I'm going to make the most of it. When you see the great outlook they have, you realize what's really important."

Long before his elbow gave out, Motte had grasped the importance of family, faith, and helping others. He became so attached to his daughter, Margaret, after she was born on January 7, 2013, that Caitlin said he hardly allowed her to change diapers. When the day neared to report to Jupiter, Florida, and Margaret a month old, Motte decided he couldn't go to the Sunshine State without her. "She came down to spring training because I wasn't ready to [leave her] yet," he said. "I prayed about it. *I don't know how I'm going to get through this. God, just give me strength to get through this.* He's got a sense of humor. *You want to spend more time with your family? I got you covered.* I got the message."

When many pro athletes start their foundation, their first order of business is to appoint a staff. They want someone to run the show and deal with the public they're aiming to help, someone to do the work. The Jason Motte Foundation is run by a staff of two: Jason and Caitlin. "We are very hands on people," Caitlin says. "If we were going to do this, we want to be as involved as we can. We didn't want to just have it in name only. We want to make the decisions, not have anyone make them for us. This is a cause that is near and dear to us."

"There are a lot of impressive guys in the league, and some of them are more visible to the public in that way. Jason is among the top," says Tim Slavin, an executive with the MLB Players Association. "He's not the guy who sits in some corner office. He's the guy who is down there on the line working with everybody, pushing the balls forward to make sure everything works well and that everyone is happy."

The Mottes' cause is as straightforward as one of Jason's fastballs. "We want to do anything we can to help make things easier on cancer patients and their families," Caitlin said. "All funds we raise go to helping [cancer] research and providing comfort and care. That's our current and our long-term goal."

They formed the Jason Motte Foundation after Caitlin's grandfather, Lynn Doyle, was diagnosed with lung cancer in 2010, and the Mottes asked what they could do to help. Little did they know how it would grow. Their main fundraiser, a Strike Out Cancer event held during November in Memphis, where they live, raised upward of $100,000 in two years and moved into a larger facility in year three. They introduced their "Cornhole Challenge"—a beanbag tossing contest for charity—in St. Louis last summer.

When nurses at St. Louis' Cardinal Glennon Children's Medical Center had a patient who needed cheering up, they didn't need to set up a visit from Motte through a PR firm. They have Jason's cell phone number, and he's told them to use it. There were times that summer of 2013 when Motte dropped what he was doing and headed for a hospital. On one occasion Cardinal Glennon nurse Kate Kozemczak remembers that Motte showed up only to learn the patient had been transferred to another hospital. Motte turned around and made the visit. "It is all about trying to help as many people as we can," Motte said. "That is what it's all about for us."

Young Brandt Ballenger didn't care that Motte pitched for the Cardinals. Truth be told, Brandt had not heard of Motte until a photograph showed up on the youngster's Facebook page of the bearded pitcher holding a "Team Brandt" sign. To Brandt, who suffered from pediatric kidney cancer, they were just a couple of guys who liked video games. "Jason was his friend who would visit to play Chutes and Ladders," said Robin Ballenger, Brandt's mom.

Motte visited Brandt often at Cardinal Glennon in the spring 2013 where the youngster would have his cancer treated. They had met in Orlando during spring training that year on Brandt's Make-A-Wish trip to Disney World. A few weeks later, Motte invited Brandt to ride with him in the players' parade around Busch Stadium on Opening Day. A friendship was born between the pitcher, who closed out the 2011 World Series, and the young boy, who was diagnosed with kidney cancer the next day.

After their Opening Day ride, Motte began to visit Brandt often at Cardinal Glennon and at the youngster's home in Swansea, Illinois. For the next few months, until Brandt died on July 23, 2013, the irrepressible young patient and the unruly-bearded dude Brandt nicknamed "Hobo" made an unlikely but special couple. Motte became such a regular at Cardinal Glennon visiting Brandt that he grew to be friends with some of the doctors and nurses. That led to visiting other patients, and Motte came to fully appreciate the difference he could make by taking a few minutes out of his day for others. "After he passed away, the nurses came to the field and said, 'Man, he loved you,'" Motte said. "I said, 'Yeah.' They said, 'No, you don't understand. If you came on Friday and said you were coming back on Monday, he would talk about Friday all day Friday and Saturday. And he would talk about Monday all day Sunday and Monday until you came.'"

When he's not in a baseball uniform, Motte's left wrist typically is covered with bracelets he wears in support of his young friends, and "I have about 40 more in my truck," he said. "This platform that we're given, you can use it for good or you can use it to be an idiot," Motte said. "What a lot of people don't know is that a lot of people do more good than bad. It's great to show that guys do stuff like this, but that's not why I'm doing this. I might only be here a short time. If I can raise awareness and money for other people, why would I not use that platform for good?"

Hometown Boy Steps Up

The night before Game 6 of the 2011 World Series, David Freese spent the evening like a typical bachelor. He dined out with friends, stayed up late, and crashed on a buddy's sofa. Who would have thought then that his life would be changed forever before his next work day was over? Who would have thought in his next game he would produce one of the most dramatic moments in World Series history? Who would have thought he was just a day away from becoming a legend in his hometown?

Freese merely was sticking to a routine that had worked rather well all that October. He already had won the Most Valuable Player in the National League Championship Series and was well on the way to breaking the record for most RBIs in a postseason. Because the place in St. Louis' Central West End he was moving into late that summer was not yet equipped for cable TV, Freese started staying at a college friend's apartment in nearby Brentwood. As the Cardinals went on their late-season roll for the ages, superstition took over. The small sofa that Freese used as a bed wasn't the most comfortable resting place for a 6'2", 225-pound man, but he wasn't about to test the baseball gods. He was running on adrenaline anyway, so sleep would have been hard to come by no matter where he put down his head.

When rain forced Game 6 to be postponed from Wednesday to Thursday night, all Freese wanted was a night of normalcy. The more runs he had driven in that month, the more attention was heaped on the young man who grew up in a St. Louis suburb in a home full of

Cardinals fans. After losing a bizarre Game 5 at Texas on Monday night, the Cardinals had returned to Busch Stadium needing a victory in Game 6 just to send the series to a seventh game. When rain washed out the game on Wednesday, both teams were left to deal with a ballplayer's worst foe at that late date in the postseason: idle time.

But by being in familiar digs and kicking back with his buddies, Freese could count on an easy evening. He had only one hit in the previous two games and wanted to ease his mind a bit. The group headed out to a nondescript Mexican restaurant tucked in a strip mall off the Delmar Loop, and then it was back to his buddy's place to hang out and rest up.

When later I talked to Freese about his fairy tale month, he said being at home for those final two games was a huge benefit that was enhanced even more by the rainout. While the Cardinals were able to chill out on their home turf, the Rangers had two days with little to do but wait for the World Series to resume. Adding to the challenge, many of the Rangers had not played in St. Louis before the World Series and were not familiar with the city. "We didn't have to sit around staring at the ceiling in the hotel, mulling over Game 6," Freese said. "We were with our families and friends. Everybody was able to take a breather and relax. A lot of guys saw friends and family that night, which might have gotten their minds off the situation. You're able to live a lifestyle you're accustomed to, whether you don't mind staying in a hotel or not. There is a difference to it."

Whether it was the previous night's burritos at Mi Ranchito or the extra day of down time, something—eventually—clicked for Freese and the Cardinals the next night. St. Louis started Game 6 like it was going to hand the championship to the Rangers. Starter Jaime Garcia lasted only three innings, reliever Lance Lynn gave up back-to-back homers, and the Cardinals made three errors, one of them by Freese when he dropped a pop-up that most little leaguers would have caught. "I felt like I was part of a circus," he said. "But man, I just wanted an opportunity."

He would get his wish before the end of the four-hour, 33-minute contest played on a cold October night. The Rangers used a three-run seventh inning to break a 4–4 tie and send the clubhouse attendants scurrying to prepare for a champagne celebration. Allen Craig hit a one-out homer in the eighth to keep the Cardinals' hopes alive, but they entered the bottom of the ninth down by two runs and having to take on Neftali Feliz, the young Rangers closer who had not allowed a hit or a run in his three previous outings.

Feliz wasted little time getting the first out, striking out Ryan Theriot with a fastball timed at 98 mph. But Albert Pujols doubled to center field, Lance Berkman walked on four pitches, and Busch Stadium began to rock. Then Craig watched a slider zip past him for called strike three, and the Rangers were one out from their first World Series championship.

Up came Freese, hitless in the game and facing Feliz for the first time in his career. Freese took a slider for ball one, watched another for a called strike, and then whiffed on a 98 mph fastball. With the season down to its last strike, Feliz delivered another 98 mph heater.

Freese did not whiff on this one.

Known for his opposite-field thumb, he drove the ball deep to right field, and because right fielder Nelson Cruz was not stationed deep enough, it sailed over his head and out of his reach. The ball bounced off the fence, two runs scored, and Freese ended up on third with the biggest hit of his life to that point. "I went to the dish and told myself to just stay short," Freese said. "He started me off with some off-speed, so I was like, *Now what's coming?* I said heater and I just looked for something out over the plate. I swung through one and then got the same kind of pitch. I didn't miss that one."

The Rangers, though, weren't done. They took the lead in the 10th on a two-run homer by Josh Hamilton, but the Cardinals, one strike from the end for the second time, tied the game again when Berkman singled up the middle to drive in the equalizer. With pitching starting to

David Freese hits a walk-off home run in the 11th inning against Texas Rangers pitcher Mark Lowe to win Game 6 of the 2011 World Series.

run short on both sides, the Cardinals sent out starter Jake Westbrook for the 11th inning, and he held the Rangers scoreless. Texas countered in the bottom of the inning with Mark Lowe, a hard-throwing right-hander who had pitched only once in the series, a mop-up inning in the Cardinals' 16–7 Game 3 victory.

Freese led off for the Cardinals and watched Lowe throw three straight balls. The Rangers reliever then battled back with two strikes on 96 and 95 mph fastballs. This time, Lowe tried his first change-up, but it didn't fool Freese. He knocked the ball over the center-field wall for a home run that created as many goose bumps as any in the storied history of the Cardinals. "I was worried about getting on base leading off an inning, and a full count came," Freese said. "I knew he had a good change-up. So I kind of had that in the back of my head." The home run was a moon shot. "I saw the usher trying to keep everybody off the grass but that obviously didn't work," he said.

By the time Freese returned to his buddy's place after the game, midnight had long passed, and sleep would be even harder to come by. He says he caught maybe a 45-minute nap before giving up and heading to a nearby McDonald's for his postseason breakfast burrito. "I felt rested," he said. "I was fired up."

The next night in Game 7, he provided his heroics in his first at-bat when he doubled in two runs to even the game after the Rangers had taken an early lead. Craig hit a bases-empty home run in the third that broke the tie, and from there the Cardinals cruised to a 6–2 victory and secured the franchise's 11th championship.

That night, Freese slept at his own place.

* * *

The road to becoming a hometown hero was not always smooth for Freese. During 2009 he had been arrested for driving while intoxicated after he was stopped in the middle of the night for driving the wrong way down a four-lane road in the suburbs. This was his third encounter with the police that involved alcohol since he had graduated from Lafayette High School in 2001. The next day Cardinals general manager John Mozeliak let him know a fourth misstep would not be tolerated.

Freese had not spoken publicly about his arrest, which was even bigger news in St. Louis than the usual offense of a professional athlete because of his roots. He was one of the few players on the team to live in the area year-round, too. The Winter Warm-Up would be the first time Freese had spoken publicly since the arrest. A uniquely Cardinals event, the Warm-up is a three-day event where fans pack a downtown hotel to stand in line for up to two hours to pay as much as $150 for autographs (proceeds go to Cardinals' charities) and hopefully rub shoulders with their favorite Cardinals past and present.

Before the players make their two-hour appearance to sign autographs, they are ushered into a side room by the team's media relations staff to talk with the media. Questions typically are decidedly softball. New players are asked how excited they are to play for the Cardinals; returning players are queried about their offseason vacations.

This year was different. The team's new batting coach, Mark McGwire, was scheduled to make his first public appearance since his nationally televised news conference during which he admitted using steroids. McGwire had agreed to talk about the past at the request of the Cardinals, who were taking a chance on hiring the disgraced slugger. Because of McGwire's expected appearance, national media outlets had descended on the Hyatt Regency Saint Louis at the Arch as well as all the local outlets.

McGwire went out to center stage at the very time Freese was led into his own news conference. With so much interest in McGwire, the team's media relations representatives accompanied the former slugger to the big room and left Freese alone with reporters. When the PR folks are on hand, these press conferences usually last no more than 10 minutes. With no one to protect Freese, a few of us grilled him for more than 20 minutes. *Was he still drinking? Did he believe he had a drinking problem? How did the club handle his arrest?* We went on so long that I began to look around to see if someone from the club was coming back to give him a break.

Freese answered every question—even the ones asked two or three times—with the professionalism of a 10-year veteran, not an unproven rookie who had spent only a few weeks in the major leagues. He had entered the club's employee assistance program. He had stopped drinking. He also had lost 15 pounds in a month while dropping his body-fat percentage to ensure that he entered spring training as ready as possible. "I've sat around for long days the past few weeks and thought about where I'm at and what kind of opportunity I've had," he told us. "A lot of kids would dream to be in the position I'm in. I take full responsibility for my actions. I don't feel I have an addiction problem, but when things like that happen, you're going to take the necessary steps to make sure they don't happen again. That's what I've done. I'm not drinking right now. I don't know what the future holds, but taking this one day at a time is what I'm going to do. For sure, when you make mistakes, you're going to have to regain the credibility and trust of the organization. Bottom line, they're trying to win as many games as they can and they're going to put the best team out there. My off-the-field issues are something I'm taking care of. The Cardinals are obviously watching that. I'm really pumped and excited about where I am. I haven't felt this good in a long time physically and mentally."

Freese carried that good vibe into spring training and, as was projected, won the starting job at third base. He got off to a strong start, too, and was hitting .316 when he hurt his right ankle in early June. He played with the injury for a few weeks before his season ended June 27 and he ended up undergoing reconstructive surgery.

Unfortunately, he had been dealing with injuries long before he signed his first contract. In 2003, while at junior college, he broke both of his wrists in a pick-up basketball game. After he joined the Cardinals, he seemed to be hurt more often than he was healthy. Freese missed much of the 2009 season with foot injuries suffered when his car slipped off an icy road in the offseason. In 2011 he was hit by a pitch that broke his left hand and cost him nearly two months. He bruised his back trying to catch a foul pop in spring training 2013 and did not completely recover all season. Even in 2012, the lone season when he avoided the disabled list, various ailments caused him to miss 18 games. Still, Freese made the All-Star team, hit a career-best 20 home runs, and—for the most part—was able to meet the expectations created by his 2011 postseason.

Expectations also were nothing new for Freese. When he was a senior in high school, he was considered one of the best players in Missouri but decided not to play in college because he was burned out on the game. Not even fellow Lafayette alum Ryan Howard could talk him out of giving up the game. Freese went to Missouri and enjoyed a freshman year with no practicing but plenty of chances for partying.

That next summer, however, he changed his mind again. Freese was home working for the local school district when he decided to resume playing. He attended a local junior college for two years before heading to South Alabama, where the American Coaches Association named him the country's top third baseman in 2006. The year off probably saved his career. "If I didn't quit for that year, I don't think I would be playing today," he said. "If I had done what everyone else had told me to do—to not quit—I think I would've been burnt out even more. That one year made me understand that baseball was a big part of me, and I found the love for it again."

The Cardinals traded Jim Edmonds for Freese in 2007 because they liked his power potential and his glove at third. The acquisition would pay off for the club and the player with his record postseason in 2011 and his All-Star campaign in 2012. But he started 2013 on the disabled list because of the back injury and he struggled all season to find his power at the plate. He lost his job briefly in August and he delivered little magic in the Cardinals' run to the World Series. He did not have an RBI or score a run while hitting 3-for-19 against the Boston Red Sox.

When the Cardinals traded him weeks later to the Los Angeles Angels, Mozeliak admitted the hoopla that goes with being a hometown hero might have caught up to Freese. "For David, this could not have been the easiest place to play," Mozeliak said. "This was not an easy year for him." The comments bothered Freese, who insisted his off year was nothing more than "growing pains being in the big leagues." "I need to hone in and be me," he added. "Just do what I do. The last thing I'm worried about is if I'm going to hit."

He couldn't be too upset with his hometown team. The Cardinals gave him his chance to play in the big leagues and he returned the favor with a moment that will never be forgotten in his hometown. "Let's be honest," he told mlb.com early in the 2014 season. "You can't beat that."

Only 31, Freese has a lot of baseball left, but from the day he was traded, he already was looking forward to the day when he would be asked to throw out a ceremonial first pitch as have so many of the club's former stars. "When I'm 60," he added with a smile.

Playing Through Pain

David Freese had the hometown hero angle working for him in the 2011 World Series, but an even more dramatic backstory accompanied Allen Craig's heroics. Craig was quite a standout, too. He hit three home runs and drove in a run in all of the Cardinals' victories, including the winner in Games 1 and 7. Pretty impressive for someone playing with a broken leg, wouldn't you say?

"Well, not exactly a broken leg," Craig said.

Okay, then what? "A broken bone in my kneecap."

Oh, that's all. The break was serious enough that Craig underwent surgery weeks following the World Series to have two screws inserted to secure his right patella, a procedure that cost him the first month of the 2012 season.

Semantics aside, no one doubts that Craig had played the 2011 post-season at considerably less than 100 percent. Not only was his kneecap fractured from a collision with the wall in Houston's Minute Maid Park, but his right leg remained weak from two months of inactivity. "I lost a lot of strength in my quad and legs because when there's a lot of swelling in your knee, your body tells your quad to shut down. That, combined with the swelling, was why it took so long for the rehab," he told me later. "They weren't going to let me play if my quad is shut down because you risk injuries like ACL and MCL."

But even at less than his best, Craig was able to do what he does best, which is drive in big runs. He did not play much in the first two rounds but had contributed a home run and gone 2-for-4 as a pinch-hitter in the National League Championship Series. It was during the World Series when his reputation as a clutch hitter really began to flourish.

In St. Louis' 3–2 victory in Game 1, Craig was called on to pinch hit for Chris Carpenter with two outs in the sixth inning of a tie game and lined a single to right that brought home the winning run. Rangers manager Ron Washington had hoped his team would benefit from walking No. 8 hitter Nick Punto to force Carpenter from the game at a time when the Cardinals' ace was dealing. After Craig was announced, Washington lifted his starter, lefty C.J. Wilson, in favor of hard-throwing right-hander Alexi Ogando. Featuring a 100 mph fastball, Ogando had dominated in the playoffs for the Rangers by allowing only one run in seven appearances while striking out 12.

Because Craig had sat on the bench for two hours on a chilly night, the challenge of facing Ogando was even greater than usual. Trying to hit a 100 mph heater on a cold, windy night is not fun or easy. Craig whiffed on 96 and 97 mph heaters and fell behind in the count 1–2. "I wasn't overwhelmed. I just missed them," Craig said later. "I had to make an adjustment. I had to keep it a little more simple and not try to hit it so hard. I wanted to put the ball in play. Good things happen when you put the ball in play."

Craig certainly put the next pitch—a fastball timed at 98 mph—in play. He sliced it down the right-field line for a single. "I didn't know it was a hit until he picked it up and threw it in," Craig said. "He made an unbelievable effort. I thought he caught it." After rounding first, Craig had to duck to keep Nelson Cruz's throw from hitting him on the way back to the base.

The Rangers had two pinch-hitting chances in the next inning after putting two runners on with one out, but neither Craig Gentry nor Esteban German were able to put the ball in play against the St. Louis bullpen. "Their pinch-hitter got it done, and ours didn't," Washington said in the postgame news conference. "Give them credit."

- In Game 2, Craig broke a scoreless tie in the seventh with a pinch-hit single to right but the Rangers rallied for a 2–1 victory.
- In Game 3, Craig slugged a first-inning home run, but it was reduced to a footnote thanks to Albert Pujols, who triggered a 16–7 victory with his historic, three-homer, five-hit effort.
- In Game 6, Craig supplied an eighth-inning homer that cut Texas' three-run deficit to 7–5 and set the stage for Freese's heroics.
- In Game 7, Freese tied the score with a two-run double in the first before Craig delivered a homer in the third that put the Cardinals ahead for good. Craig was in the lineup only because Matt Holliday was out with an injury. Craig also took a home run

away from Cruz with a catch in the sixth inning and was in left field to secure the final out of the World Series on a fly by David Murphy.

Craig finished the Series with five hits, five runs, and five RBIs and was the Cardinals' only player to drive in a run in as many as five games. The showing was impressive by any standards but particularly for someone on a bad leg who had missed two months during the regular season. The Cardinals initially called it a bone bruise, but a few days later, the injury was diagnosed as a fracture in his kneecap. Craig opted against surgery and spent his time on the disabled list strengthening the muscles around his injured knee and hoping the fracture would heal. He was cleared to return when he passed a series of strength tests, even though the bone was not quite healed. "It was sore and it got real stiff and it was something that forced me to take extra time to warm up," he said. "I was to the point where I wasn't risking further injury. I was playing well and wasn't hurting the team so I just kept playing."

Hitting .336 when he was hurt in June, Craig hit .290 with seven homers in 35 games after he returned. When the fracture still hadn't healed by the end of the World Series, he decided surgery would be best for his future. "This was not something you could play with over the course of a full season," he said.

Craig sat out the opening month of 2012 but quickly established himself as a regular by hitting .373 in May. He finished the season with 92 RBIs, even though he missed 43 games. He would be even better in 2013. Craig signed a five-year contact extension in spring training, made his first All-Star team, and had piled up 96 RBIs entering September. He would not get to 100, though, after he suffered a left foot injury when he was rounding first base after a hit in Cincinnati on September 4.

Craig would not play again until the World Series, when once again he found himself in the middle of some drama that had his teammates likening him to the Dodgers' Kirk Gibson in 1988. With one out, one on, and the score 4–4 in the bottom of the ninth of Game 3, Craig was called on to pinch hit against Koji Uehara. The Red Sox closer had been the game's most unhittable pitcher in the second half in large part due to a devastating split-finger fastball. Uehara had posted a 0.28 ERA after the All-Star break while sporting a 41-strikeout-to-one-walk ratio in 32 innings.

His first pitch to Craig, though, was not a splitter but an 88 mph fastball that Craig laced into the left-field corner for a double. For a guy who barely could walk without a limp, that was worthy of being mentioned with Gibson. Craig's hit advanced Yadier Molina to third and set the stage for one of the most bizarre endings to a World Series game. With Molina representing the winning run and Craig on second, the Red Sox moved the infield in for Jon Jay, and he grounded sharply to second baseman Dustin Pedroia, who threw out Molina at the plate.

But instead of settling for just one out, catcher Jarrod Saltalamacchia got greedy and tried to throw out Craig at third. The throw went a little wide of the base, and when third baseman Will Middlebrooks lunged to make the catch, the ball darted away as Craig slid in. With the ball rolling around, Craig got up and took off for home only to stumble over the fallen Middlebrooks. Craig chugged away, anyway, stumbling as you'd expect for someone running on a bad ankle and he was tagged when he made an awkward slide at the plate.

Only Craig wasn't out.

Third-base umpire Jim Joyce had called obstruction on Middlebrooks for tripping Craig, which allowed him to take home safely and give the Cardinals a walk-off win on an umpire's interference call. Craig did not even know he was safe until "I saw my entire team running out on the field."

Though many of his teammates said they didn't know exactly what happened, they rushed the plate as soon as they saw that Craig had been called safe. They came to mob him but let up when they saw he was hurting. Craig had to be helped off the field and to the trainer's room, where he spent more than half an hour receiving treatment. When he came through the clubhouse, he wasn't limping, but neither was he moving comfortably. "Kirk Gibson-esque," teammate Matt Carpenter said. "That was gutsy base running there on a real bad ankle. You can't say enough about him. He's banged up, not even close to 100 percent. He could have taken it easier and protected his body. He went all out and we won the game." When told that a teammate had likened him to Gibson, Craig shook his head. "Oh man, don't do that to me," he said. "I was just trying to make a play...I feel okay, a little sore. Trying to get home, I didn't have much in the tank to be honest with you. That's probably the fastest I've tried to run in the past two months."

Although the play was crazy, it was called correctly. "Obstruction is the act of a fielder obstructing a runner when not in the act of fielding a ball," umpire crew chief John Hirschbeck said. "There does not have to be intent." Added Joyce, "When he tried to advance to home plate, the feet were up in the air, and he tripped over Middlebrooks and immediately and instinctually I called obstruction."

"I could tell [something happened]," Craig said. "I had to try to jump over him. I don't know if he clipped me or not it happened so fast." Craig entered the series just thankful to have an opportunity to play after suffering a Lisfranc injury when he turned his ankle after getting a hit in Cincinnati. "This is what you live for, to be able to contribute in World Series games," Craig said. "I'm glad I got the opportunity to bat in the bottom of the ninth inning in Game 3 of the World Series."

Drafted out of Cal in 2006, Craig hit well at every minor-league stop but had to bide his time waiting for big-league at-bats. He reached the majors in 2010 and emerged as a fourth outfielder and later, a World Series hero in 2011.

As Freese was gallivanting across the land as a national celebrity for his postseason exploits following the Cardinals' 11th World Series title, Craig settled for a smaller spotlight. In his hometown of Temecula, California, he became the first baseball player to have his jersey retired at Chaparral High School. There were presentations on the baseball field and an assembly in front of the student body. The native Southern Californian also was presented with his own day complete with a key to the city. "That was all cool," Craig said. "To be the first guy and to have the whole school there was real humbling."

Berkman's Comeback

If not for David Freese, Lance Berkman could have made a deserving MVP in the 2011 World Series. If not for Albert Pujols' sensational second half, Berkman could have made an obvious MVP for the Cardinals during the regular season. As it turned out, Berkman was named the National League Comeback Player of the Year and also was voted by Cardinals players as the winner of the Darryl Kile Award for being a great teammate.

His first season in St. Louis was that special and was topped, of course, by his performance in the World Series. Berkman set a Cardinals' franchise World Series record by scoring nine runs, and his 11 hits were the most by a Cardinal in a World Series since Lou Brock collected 12 in 1967. Berkman hit .423 against the Texas Rangers and reached base 16 times in 31 plate appearances.

In Game 6 he went 3-for-5 with a homer, scored four runs, and drove in three, including the tying run in the ninth inning. After the Rangers went ahead by two in the 10th, Berkman tied the game with a two-out, two-strike single that followed an intentional walk to Pujols. Afterward, in a display of candor not seen often in professional athletes, Berkman said what many players must feel but rarely admit. "I don't think this is fun," he said. "I mean, it's obviously fun when you win, but going into the game it's not fun. It's not fun to go up there with a season on the line. But the experience is incredible."

Berkman was not too proud to admit that he sought help before his broken-bat hit evened the score and set the stage for Freese's walk-off homer in the next inning. "I don't pray for hits and stuff like that, but I definitely prayed for a calmness and an ability to compete at a high level that I'm capable of," he said. "The tendency in these big situations, your emotions get going, you try to do too much. If you're a .300 hitter, all you can reasonably expect to do in big situations is hit .300. I mean, you can't be better than you are."

If he had not come through in the 10th inning, Berkman said he would've gone home to spend time with the family and wouldn't have had time to worry about failing in the clutch. "I actually felt pretty good about it because I figured I was in a no-lose situation," he said. "They might talk about it for a couple days, but it's not that big a deal. If you come through, it's the greatest. Plus, you've built a little bank account of being able to come through. If I don't come through [in Game 7], I can be like, 'Well, I came through in Game 6, what do you want from me?'"

Berkman delivered in Game 7, too, scoring twice in the 6–2 clinching victory. When he lifted Tony La Russa in a massive bear hug after the final out, it marked an incredible end to his first World Series championship that had come one year after the worst season of his 15-year career. Berkman had played like a guy whose career was winding down in a hurry in 2010 after he returned too early from spring training knee surgery. The only team he had played on, the Houston Astros, traded him to the New York Yankees, where he served as a backup outfielder for the stretch drive. His .248 batting average for the season was 45 points off his career mark, and his 14 homers were the fewest since his 1999 rookie season.

I remember being in the Yankees clubhouse after they had lost to the Rangers in the American League Championship Series. Berkman seemed more likely to retire than to end up in St. Louis, a place where he had endured his share of disappointments when he was with the Astros. But Cardinals general manager John Mozeliak did not believe Berkman was finished before turning 35. Even though the Cardinals were set at first base with a guy named Pujols, Mozeliak pursued Berkman to play right field. The Chicago Cubs came close to landing him to be their first baseman, but after the Cardinals offered $4 million, Berkman told St. Louis if the team upped it to $8 million with no incentives, he wouldn't bother with the Cubs. The signing proved to be a bargain for the Cardinals.

Berkman started strongly and emerged as the National League's top slugger in the first half with 24 homers and a .602 slugging percentage. The production was needed even more than expected because Pujols started slowly, and Matt Holliday missed considerable time with injuries. Besides his on-the-field contributions, Berkman also lifted the mood of a clubhouse that needed an injection of happy with his Texas twang, quick wit, and veteran presence. The Cardinals had wanted Berkman for his personality almost as much as for his playing ability, and he didn't disappoint. His locker at Busch Stadium was located between those of Holliday and Pujols. With neither of the mainstays particularly forthcoming with the media, Berkman quickly became an unofficial team spokesman and media favorite. He fit in even better with his teammates.

When Ryan Franklin blew four of his first five save chances and the Cardinals started 2–6 in 2011, Berkman was the man who lifted spirits in the clubhouse. When Matt Carpenter would emerge as an everyday player in 2012, Berkman would be giving him a hard time about having his wife, Mackenzie, continue to hold her teaching job. When laughter erupted inside the clubhouse, often it was because of a punch line delivered by Berkman.

Berkman also was playing with the added motivation of proving that he wasn't finished, that he still was an elite player. In the offseason after signing with St. Louis, Berkman retained a personal trainer for the first time and strengthened his knees and lost 20 pounds. He arrived in spring training ready to play right field, claiming that the position would be easier on his legs than playing first base. The notion that a position requiring a great deal of running would be less stressful than standing around the infield seemed silly—but not to Berkman. "At first base there's a tremendous amount of direction change. There's stopping and starting. You're holding guys on. You're bouncing off. You're having to get back," he said. "In right you run from A to B and either catch the ball or don't get there. That's easy if your legs are in good shape."

Berkman often thought outside the box, at least outside of the established baseball box. During his two years in St. Louis, I had numerous chances to talk with him, and he seldom failed to enlighten and entertain. On the often-discussed topic of speeding up the time it takes to play a game, Berkman offered a radical suggestion: "If you want to shorten the game, you have to shorten the game. You can't play nine innings. Shorten it to seven innings and then it will be a two-and-a-half hour game or a two-hour game. The little Mickey Mouse stuff they try to do to speed the game that cuts 15 seconds here or there, that's not going to shorten the game appreciably. Even if it shortens the game five minutes or 10 minutes, who cares about that? I hate long games. It wears on you after a while." When I ran Berkman's idea past Bud Selig later that season, the then-commissioner smiled. "Lance has had a great year, but that isn't one of his best ideas," he said.

On the differences in the National League and the American League, Berkman said, "The DH makes a big difference. You make that pitcher hit and now you have an automatic rally-killer that doesn't prolong some of those innings. That's one reason the National League is shorter and better. I don't like the American League game. It's not really baseball, at least not from a strategy standpoint of having to make a decision [about] do we leave pitcher in or take him out. It's just based on whether he's tired or not. There's no double-switching that makes the game to me interesting."

On the baseball record book: "The problem is a lot of the 'records,' like the 56-game hitting streak, are just not possible now because the competition is so much better. The game has changed so much that it's not even the same game. There were no African Americans. There were no Latin players. It was a very small talent pool and it was all white guys…No one is going to hit .400 ever again unless they do something drastic like move the mound back. There's a reason no one has done it for so long. There are too many specialists, too many guys that throw too hard now. People talk all they want about how Bob Feller threw 100 [mph]. I just don't believe that. Even if there were guys who threw close to that hard, there were one or two, not one or two on every team."

Berkman left the Cardinals after an injury-filled 2012 season and signed with the Rangers. When the Rangers visited St. Louis for an interleague series during the season, Berkman was welcomed back as a conquering hero. Everyone wanted to know: had he gloated about beating his new teammates in the 2011 World Series? More than once, he said.

It started during spring training when Rangers manager Ron Washington was giving his preseason speech. "What he said was we have a lot of guys that have been through the war," Berkman recalled. "He was going down the list of names. Ian Kinsler, you've been through the war; David Murphy, you've been through the war; Berkman, you've been through the war. I was like, 'We won that war, Wash.' It probably got their goat a little bit."

La Russa's Last Run

Perhaps the baseball world should not have been stunned when Tony La Russa retired from managing the Cardinals three days after they won the 2011 World Series. The man had dropped enough clues in the preceding weeks that anyone around the club should have picked up that something was going on. For a manager best known for his intensity, La Russa appeared far more relaxed than usual during the Cardinals' remarkable stretch drive and postseason run. He smiled at times when you expected the cold-hard stare. He even seemed to enjoy talking with the media, particularly veteran baseball writers. "I saw him smile more in the last few months during baseball games than I ever saw in the eight years I was here before," Chris Carpenter said the morning after La Russa's announcement. "Now I know why."

Look at how he handled the bullpen mix-up in Game 5 of the World Series, when somehow he ended up with a reliever on the mound who was not supposed to pitch that day. Considering the snafu led to the Texas Rangers' winning runs and put the Cardinals in a 3–2 hole, his patience with answering the same questions being asked over and over was remarkable. This was a man who had no problem letting a reporter know when he had asked a dumb question.

La Russa explained what went wrong in his news conference following the game. He talked about what had happened the next day during an off-day presser typically held to look ahead to the next game. Not long after that formal session, La Russa talked about the mistake yet again with a handful of reporters who had lingered outside of his office after the Cardinals clubhouse had closed to the media. No matter how many times he heard the same questions, he replied like he was answering for the first time. Considering how costly and bizarre the glitch had been, it was easy to understand why the media kept asking about it. La Russa understood this. Still, admitting to mistakes that might have cost his team a World Series game couldn't have been enjoyable.

The game was tied going into the bottom of the eighth, and La Russa pulled the starter, Carpenter, for Octavio Dotel. Dotel promptly gave up a double but then struck out Adrian Beltre.

With first base open, an intentional walk was ordered against Nelson Cruz, a dangerous power hitter. Pitching coach Dave Duncan visited the mound, and Dotel said he would have no problem issuing a free pass and he did.

La Russa, meanwhile, had called the bullpen to have left-hander Marc Rzepczynski warm up and right-hander Jason Motte to play catch. Bullpen coach Derek Lilliquist, however, heard Rzepczynski but he didn't hear Motte. Rzepczynski got up but, unbeknownst to La Russa, Motte did not. After Dotel issued the intentional walk, La Russa brought in Rzepczynski to face lefty-hitting David Murphy. So far, so good.

Around this time, the skipper also had noticed that Motte wasn't warming so he called the bullpen again. Only this time, Lilliquist heard "Lynn" instead of "Motte." Even though Lance Lynn was supposed to be used only in an emergency situation, Lilliquist got him up. Hey, eighth inning of a close game in the World Series could be considered an emergency. La Russa was hoping that Rzepczynski would retire Murphy so the Cardinals could pitch around the next hitter, dangerous right-hander Mike Napoli, and Rzepczynski could go after another lefty hitter, the struggling Mitch Moreland. Rzepczynski got Murphy to hit a grounder right back at the pitcher that looked like an apparent double-play ball, but the ball deflected off his glove and went for an infield single. Now the bases were loaded with Napoli coming up.

This was the very situation for which La Russa wanted Motte to be ready, but Motte had not yet thrown a single warm-up pitch. La Russa did not see a way to stall long enough for Motte to warm up in time to face Napoli, so he had no choice but to have a lefty face a hitter who was known for pounding lefties. The result was almost predictable. Napoli drove a 1–1 slider to center field for a two-run double that put the Cardinals in a 4–2 hole.

Rzepczynski then struck out Moreland, and La Russa went to the mound planning to bring in Motte to face the Rangers' right-handed hitting leadoff hitter, Ian Kinsler. As La Russa walked to the mound and signaled to the umpire he wanted the right-hander, he heard the bench calling. But La Russa kept walking, only to arrive at the mound and see Lynn instead of Motte. "Why are you here," he asked Lynn.

La Russa did not want to put Lynn's right arm at risk because the rookie right-hander had thrown 47 pitches two days prior. But Lynn had to face one batter before he could be taken out of the game so La Russa had him intentionally walk Kinsler. Then, finally, he was able to summon Motte who struck out Elvis Andrus. The damage, however, had been done. When the Cardinals failed to score in the ninth, the Rangers and Cardinals were headed back to St. Louis with Texas just one win away from eliminating St. Louis. In his postgame news conference, La Russa stopped short of accepting responsibility for the breakdown. "I was more frustrated the double play ball went off [Rzepczynski's] glove and the fact we had numerous chances to add runs," La Russa said. "It's loud down there. Sometimes you call down there and you have to wait until the crowd [quiets], and a guy gets up late. I mean this is not unusual."

The bullpen breakdown wasn't the only mistake that La Russa was left to explain. In the ninth inning, with Albert Pujols batting, La Russa ordered a hit-and-run with plodding Allen Craig on first base. Only Pujols swung and missed at strike three, and Craig was thrown out trying to reach second for a double play that sealed the outcome. In the seventh, again with Craig on first, Pujols had put on the hit-and-run himself, but when the pitch sailed high, he didn't swing and Craig was caught stealing then, too. "It was a mix-up," La Russa said defensively at his postgame news conference. "On our team nobody gets thrown under the bus."

Not surprisingly, and not without reason, the media was hard on La Russa, who was not exactly a warm-and-fuzzy guy around reporters to begin with. The next day's presser had the potential to become quite contentious. But La Russa did not let that happen as he patiently tried to explain what had gone wrong the night before with the bullpen and the missed hit and runs. Before he even took questions, he offered a strong defense for allowing Pujols the authority to call for a hit and run. "Albert had the ability on this club for several years to put a hit-and-run on," La Russa said. "Whenever I've been a manager and a player has a real good feel and can handle the bat and he wanted to be able to put a play on, he's been given that right. It has everything to do with what Albert has earned as far as his understanding of the game."

When a question came about the bullpen, La Russa—before moving on—took the unusual step and asked if there were any more questions about Pujols and the hit and runs. Unlike the previous night when he downplayed the bullpen breakdown, La Russa was more frank admitting how costly it had been and accepted complete responsibility for the breakdown. "It directly affected the outcome," he said. "The stuff that went on in that inning with the bullpen and who's up and who's not, that's miscommunication. That comes totally on the coach or the manager. I explained yesterday what was going on and to the extent that what I wanted to have happen didn't happen. Yeah, that's my fault. I don't need to dodge that ever."

Following a second presser on the topic in less than a day, La Russa retreated to his office. Before long, though, he came into the hallway and once again addressed the night before. In front of a smaller contingent, mostly baseball writers he had known for years, he was able to clear up a few misunderstandings, and admitted just how difficult the snafu had been on him. "What a nightmare. My house of horrors," he said. He talked about that sick feeling of waiting for Motte—only to see Lynn. "Oh, no," he said. "This is not happening. This is a bad dream." But there was no escaping the rookie mistake of not checking the bullpen to make sure Motte was warming. "I never even looked so I can't make any excuse," he said. He was able to give a plausible explanation for why he even wanted his closer warming up in the eighth inning of a tie game on the road. "He was my most rested guy," he said.

Many times in previous situations when the press would harp on an unpleasant storyline (steroids, for example), La Russa would cut off the media and call for a new line of questioning but not this time. "It's such an unusual thing," he said. "Why wouldn't it be subject to extended national conversation? It's so unusual. I mean, it's never happened."

Rarely had he been so congenial with the media during such a difficult time. I walked away from the final session shaking my head, thinking that wasn't at all like the patronizing manager I had seen so many times. I was not the only one either. One national writer not based in St. Louis came up to me and wondered, "Is something going on with Tony? That wasn't at all how I expected him to handle this."

At the time I had no idea. I figured he was doing whatever he could to lessen the stress on his team. If he got all bent out of shape after an obvious misstep, his players might pick up on his tension and put undue pressure on themselves. This was, after all, the man who preached playing a "hard nine" every day. This was the man who, in postgame interviews that were shown on live TV, would be visibly upset after losses. But while La Russa often could be prickly, short, and condescending (usually he had good reason) with the media, he was available. He understood the media's role in the game and he would find time for that part of the job. His were not always the most pleasant interviews, but they were always professional and educational.

An exchange he had with an A's beat writer during La Russa's tenure in Oakland aptly captured his relationship with the media. It happened in 1992 on Christmas Eve, a day when reporters would rather not have any breaking news to cover. But that just happened to be the day when Mark McGwire agreed to a new contract, and the reporter needed La Russa's take. To get it would require calling the skipper at home, an imposition a reporter would rather avoid especially on a holiday. La Russa came to the phone without complaint, answered all the questions, and said good-bye. But even though La Russa often had dealt with this reporter, there was no "Merry Christmas," "Happy Holiday" or pleasantries of any sort. He did not have to treat the reporter with kindness and he didn't. But he did his job.

Many years later, I had a similar exchange that, looking back, was a result of my own mindlessness more than anything. I had been given a freelance assignment on La Russa's election to the Hall of Fame and was told the best way to arrange an interview was via text messaging. Knowing how busy is his schedule, I texted La Russa on the afternoon of Christmas Eve hoping to set up an interview. I just assumed—silly me—that if I reached him the day before the holiday, I could line up a time for the days following Christmas.

La Russa texted back and said he would call me tomorrow morning. *Hmm? Is the man so busy he doesn't realize tomorrow is the biggest holiday of the year? Or maybe his schedule was so full that he only had time for me on Christmas. I guess I'm pretty special.* I texted back and wrote, "cool, thank you."

Well, I ended up waiting all Christmas morning for a call that didn't come. I finally texted La Russa and asked if we could hold off until the next day. He replied promptly, writing "sure." The interview went off without a hitch the next day. He gave me all the time I needed as he tagged along with a group that was touring his Animal Rescue Foundation (ARF) headquarters in the East Bay area. The man has a remarkable memory concerning his baseball career. He accurately remembered anecdotes about people, places, and games. Or maybe he can retain so much about his past because he's read the many books written about or by him.

Anyhow, during that December 26 interview, La Russa told me that as soon as he stepped down in St. Louis he had started to miss the competition that came with managing. Not long after he was hired to run the Arizona Diamondbacks' baseball operations, he told me that he was fired up to justify the club's commitment to him. He insisted he wouldn't be managing again, but this new gig certainly would stoke the competitive juices he had missed.

After winning Game 7 of the 2011 World Series, Tony La Russa ends his Cardinals managerial career on a high note.

Pujols Takes the Money and Runs

Traditionally, the Winter Meetings close with the Rule 5 draft, a player-procurement procedure that not even serious baseball fans care much about. While certainly important for the clubs and the borderline prospects that are selected, seldom does the Rule 5 impact the following major league season. But it's a cool event because the Rule 5 is the one time when most everyone attending the Winter Meetings is actually in the same room. Because it is the final league-wide event before the holidays, once the final selection is made, many hands are shaken and season's greetings exchanged as the massive ballroom in some hotel empties, and a mass exodus to the nearest airport begins.

But the Winter Meetings didn't end with the Rule 5 draft in 2011. For the Cardinals and Angels, anyway, the action didn't really start until shortly before the Rule 5 draft. Right as the baseball world was filing into the Grand Ballroom of the Hilton Anatole in Dallas, word was spreading: Albert Pujols was going to the Angels. For a 10-year contract worth a ton of money—$254 million—Pujols was leaving the Cardinals and heading to the West Coast.

Three years later, not re-signing Pujols looks like the best move the Cardinals ever made. Pujols averaged 25 homers and just more than 91 RBIs with a .273/.332/.478 slash line in his first three seasons with the Angels. Those are solid numbers, but they are nothing like he put up in St. Louis. And his big money years are just beginning. After averaging $17 million so far in Anaheim, Pujols will be paid $24 million in 2015. And he will be given a $1 million raise annually until he maxes out at $30 million in 2021, when he will be 41 years old.

But Cardinals general manager John Mozeliak wasn't contemplating the distant future in his spacious suite that morning. Since the end of the season, Mozeliak and club chairman Bill DeWitt Jr. had been working to make Pujols a Cardinal for life. "You don't replace an Albert Pujols," DeWitt said early that week. "Sure we have depth, but we're a far better club with Albert than without him." The Cardinals so badly wanted to keep Pujols that the club's offer climbed from five years and $125 million earlier in the year to 10 years and upwards of $220 million during the Winter Meetings.

As is customary at the Winter Meetings, the general managers meet daily with their local media to brief them on whatever developments might or might not have taken place that day. Mozeliak and DeWitt had gone to Dallas believing the chances of Pujols re-upping still were strong, and by Wednesday they had no reason to think otherwise. The Miami Marlins had made a huge offer but wouldn't budge from their club policy to grant no-trade protection. That took them out of the bidding, and the Cardinals' chances seemed even better than when they had arrived.

But late Tuesday night, a buzz went around the Anatole that the Angels were making a run at Pujols. For the past few seasons, the Angels had become known as the team that couldn't land the big fish. Carl Crawford, Mark Teixeira, and Adrian Beltre all had shunned Anaheim in recent years, but new general manager Jerry Dipoto had secured the blessings of Arte Moreno to make a serious run at Pujols. Within a day and a half of his first substantial talks with the Pujols' camp, Dipoto had pulled off a stunner.

The normally unflappable Mozeliak was so shaken by the news that Thursday morning that he bailed on the Rule 5 draft, skipped out of the Anatole, and caught an early flight back to St. Louis. Dipoto landed starting pitcher C.J. Wilson shortly after completing Pujols' deal to make for quite a news conference that afternoon.

By the time Mozeliak arrived back in his Busch Stadium office, he already was regrouping. He would not need long to shift to Plan B. He held a presser that afternoon during which he expressed the club's disappointment over the loss of their franchise icon. "His 11 years here will always be known as historic," Mozeliak said. "We should all be grateful." The GM already had spoken with Pujols and added, "He looks at this as a new opportunity, a new challenge, and one that he felt was in his best interests. You have to honor that."

Even then, though, a sense of relief had tempered the Cardinals' disappointment. If Pujols had accepted their offer, the club would have been pushing its payroll limits to what Mozeliak admitted was an "uncomfortable" level. But without having to make that commitment, their world would be much different. "I was thinking about that on the airplane," Mozeliak said. "That does create flexibility...There's certainly some risk when you talk about these type of years."

Within two weeks Mozeliak had signed Carlos Beltran for two years and $26 million. Beltran would prove to be more productive in his two seasons with the Cardinals than Pujols was his first two seasons in California. The Cardinals still retain much of the financial muscle they gained when Pujols turned them down too. And as beloved as Pujols had become in St. Louis, the Cardinals did not have to worry about their fans' backlash. Public sentiment immediately and decisively favored the team over the player. Many, in fact, turned on Pujols with sudden and surprising venom. Some stores in the area that sold Cardinals gear gave away their stock of Pujols T-shirts. Fans all over the area burned their Pujols garb. To this day Pujols shirts remain a rare sight at Busch Stadium.

Pujols' wife, Deidre, took to local radio to give their side of the decision and wondered how so many could have turned against her husband so quickly. A suburban restaurant in which Pujols had a share, the Pujols 5, would have to change its name because business lagged after the decision. Still, Pujols has kept his foundation headquarters in St. Louis, and its charitable endeavors continue in the area. He has maintained his home in West County, too. But after three years, for many Cardinals' fans, Pujols still hasn't been forgiven as much as he has been forgotten.

PART V:
CARDINALS LEGENDS

Willie McGee, Jim Edmonds, Marty Marion, and Mike Shannon—2014 Cardinals HOF Class

Bob Gibson—HOF 1981

George Kissell—Excellence in Player Development Award Named After Him, 1995

Stan Musial—HOF 1969

Red Schoendienst—HOF 1989

The 2014 Hall of Fame Class

In the storied history of the Cardinals franchise, few have been more popular with teammates as well as fans than Willie McGee. His standing among fans was demonstrated again in 2014 when they voted him into the new Cardinals Hall of Fame. At the first balloting update, McGee already had taken such a commanding lead among the eight candidates that he could have made his reservations for the August 16 induction ceremony. McGee was inducted in the first class of the Cardinals Hall of Fame with Jim Edmonds, Marty Marion, and Mike Shannon.

Fellow candidate, pitcher Matt Morris, for one, was not surprised that McGee got the call. "The joke is it's going to be someone else and Willie McGee," Morris told mlb.com when the early voting results were released. "He was my idol in St. Louis [with] how he respected the game and how the fans respected him. So when I saw him on there, I was thinking it can be him and one other guy." McGee was just as beloved by the Cardinals players in the 1980s and not only because of his playing ability. "From a humility standpoint," Ozzie Smith said, "Willie is one of the best people I've ever met."

Smith and McGee both were traded to St. Louis in the offseason between the 1981 and '82 seasons. Smith came from the San Diego Padres for Garry Templeton in a deal that worked out in the Cardinals' favor. McGee arrived from the New York Yankees' system, where he had been seen by Whitey Herzog. Somehow Herzog convinced New York to give him up for reliever Bob Sykes, who never pitched in the majors after the deal. McGee arrived early in the '82 season and played in the majors for 18 years.

He played his first eight-plus and his final four seasons with the Cardinals. Not long after Herzog abruptly stepped down in 1990, the Cardinals shipped McGee to Tony La Russa's Oakland Athletics on August 29 after a game at Cincinnati. Rex Hudler, a utility infielder with the club at the time, remembers seeing grown men cry when McGee emerged from manager Joe Torre's office and informed his teammates that he had been dealt. "He was that special of a guy," Hudler said. Even though McGee spent the final month in the American League, he still won the National League batting title because he had enough at-bats to qualify before the trade. After he was moved, no one would match his .335 average.

The Cardinals brought back McGee as a free agent in 1996 after La Russa had been named manager, and he would spend his final four seasons in St. Louis. Smith retired after the '96 season and was working as a TV analyst for the 1997 home opener when McGee put on a display that epitomized his talent and his humbleness. Stepping up with two out in the bottom of the ninth of a 1–1 game, McGee hit a walk-off homer off Ugueth Urbina and triumphantly dropped the bat and thrust his arms into the air. But afterward, he felt so bad about his show of emotion that he called over to the Montreal Expos clubhouse and apologized.

McGee was all about playing the right away, which along with his talent, was why he became such a fan favorite. He did not show up opponents even if he might have wanted to on occasion.

San Francisco Giants pitcher Al Holland used to prance around the mound in a way that did not suit McGee. He thought Holland was showing up the Cardinals in the way he celebrated after every out. During a series in 1984 when Holland was with the Philadelphia Phillies and playing at Busch Stadium, McGee turned to Smith in the dugout and said, "I'm going to get him."

Three days later McGee did just that. In the bottom of the eighth inning of a game the Phillies were winning, he blasted a home run to straightaway center field at old Busch Stadium. "If you remember old Busch Stadium, that was not an easy thing to do," Smith said. "Willie simply ran around the bases like he always did—not about to show anyone up. He came back to the dugout and I said, 'You told me you were going to get him and you sure did. How did that feel?' He said, with just a hint of a grin, real good. *Real good.*"

Though that home run wasn't enough to defeat the Phillies that day, McGee would eventually win the 1985 MVP, two batting titles, three Gold Gloves, and was named to four All-Star teams during his time with the Cardinals. He also was one of the most popular players on one of the most popular Cardinals teams of all time. He has not had his No. 51 retired, though only Bud Smith has donned the number since McGee's final game in 1999. And Smith wore it only briefly.

The Cardinals are not expected to retire No. 51 unless McGee makes the Hall of Fame in Cooperstown. If he is to do that, it will have to be in voting by one of the special committees. He stayed on the Baseball Writers' Association of America (BBWAA) ballot for only two years, dropping off in 2006 when he did not receive the required 5 percent of the vote. A better self-promoter might have fared better, but that never has been or likely will be McGee's style.

As a roving instructor in the Cardinals' system these days, McGee teaches the same way. He isn't the type for fiery speeches or grand entrances in the clubhouse. He is happy to be on the backfields at 7:00 AM, working with the minor leaguers. "I love teaching," McGee said. "When you're with the young guys, you're doing more because they don't know as much. That means I can work more. On the major league side, you ask them if they want to do something. On the minor league side, you tell them to do it."

* * *

Few clubs are better at bridging the past with the present than the Cardinals. Of course, few clubs have as rich a history as the Cardinals. Even fewer have a Hall of Famer who has been part of the organization for most of the past 70 years as has Red Schoendienst.

No wonder when the club decided to open its Hall of Fame in the new Ballpark Village across from Busch Stadium in the spring of

2014, it was sure to include Schoendienst in the player selection process. Schoendienst has played alongside, managed, or coached virtually every player who has worn the Birds on the Bat since 1945.

That included the 2014 inductees who joined the 22 charter members of the new Cardinals Hall of Fame, all of whom qualified because they've made the Baseball Hall of Fame or had their numbers retired by the Cardinals. Schoendienst was a rookie second baseman the year after Marion had won MVP for the 1944 Cardinals that won the World Series. When Schoendienst managed the 1967 World Series champions, Shannon was the third baseman. When the Cardinals won the title in 1982 with McGee in center field, Schoendienst was the bench coach. And when they won in 2006 with Edmonds in center, he was a part of La Russa's staff.

Schoendienst didn't think higher of any of the new Hall of Famers than Marion, whom he calls the best shortstop he ever saw. The two formed the team's double-play combination from 1946–1950. Both made the All-Star team in four of those seasons. "He was a player. His feeling was so good he didn't style it or whatever you want to call it," Schoendienst said. "He was a gangly, long-legged guy with a great, accurate arm. He had such a good feel for the game that he always seemed to be in the right position. He was as good a shortstop as you ever want to look at."

Schoendienst believes Marion deserves to be in the Baseball Hall of Fame, but the baseball writers apparently weren't too impressed by his .263 career batting average. Marion received as much as 40 percent of the votes in his best showing on the ballot in 1970, but he came off the ballot in 1973.

When Edmonds debuts on the Cooperstown ballot in 2016, he can count on the backing of his longtime manager, La Russa. The duo had a few run-ins during Edmonds' eight-year stay in St. Louis, but what the skipper prefers to remember is the grace under pressure from his Gold Glove center fielder. The bigger the game, the better Edmonds seemed to perform.

He was never better than in the final two games of the 2004 National League Championship Series against the Houston Astros. La Russa was starting to feel the heat in St. Louis for not being able to take the Cardinals to the World Series despite regular appearances in the postseason. On consecutive nights, Edmonds made plays that ensured La Russa's Cardinals would break through with their first pennant since 1987.

In Game 6, Edmonds slugged a walk-off homer in the 12th inning off hard-throwing Dan Miceli to force a Game 7. The next night, the Astros took a first-inning lead and were threatening in the second when Edmonds made a diving catch on a line drive by Brad Ausmus that would be his signature play in St. Louis. Photographs of the catch are plastered on walls across the St. Louis area. "As soon as Ausmus hit the ball, I knew it was headed for the gap and I'm thinking we're going to be down by four runs," La Russa said. "We already trailed by a run, and they had two men on base. Right away, though, because of Jim's positioning, you could see that he got a good break. Now you're hoping he can close on it. Did he ever. He made up so much ground so quickly that, when you consider the situation, there's no doubt that was his greatest catch with the Cardinals. We're trying to win our first league championship, and Roger Clemens is pitching on the other side. If we had fallen behind by four runs, even though it was just the second inning, coming back would have been very, very difficult. That ball falls, we probably lose."

Edmonds slugged 241 homers for the Cardinals, an average of just more than 30 a season. He hit .285 with a .393 on-base percentage and a .555 slugging percentage and twice finished top five in MVP voting.

Shannon received MVP votes only once and hit a total of 68 homers in his nine seasons with the Cardinals, but he remains one of the most popular Cardinals of all time. In fact, he made the team's Hall of Fame mainly for what he's done since his playing career ended prematurely because of a kidney illness. Now 75, Shannon has worked as a radio play-by-play man since 1972 and has been considered the voice of the

Cardinals since Jack Buck died in 2002. "Mike's trying to carry on what Dizzy Dean did and others such as Harry Caray have done so well, but he has no visions of grandeur," said John Rooney, his broadcast partner since 2006. "Mike carries on the tradition as Mike Shannon, and that's why everybody loves him."

Though Shannon has gained his fame since he stopped playing, his athletic career should not be overlooked. He was athletic enough to play third base as well as the outfield and was considered to have one of the best arms among big league outfielders in the 1960s. Baseball might not have been his best sport either. As a St. Louis schoolboy, he was named the Missouri Player of the Year in football and basketball.

Shannon went to the University of Missouri to play football and performed so well as a freshman quarterback that the coach, Frank Broyles, later said he could have been a Heisman Trophy winner. But Shannon stayed at Missouri for only one year before he accepted a $50,000 offer to sign with the Cardinals in 1958.

He reached the majors in '62 but didn't really establish himself until he hit a home run off Whitey Ford that proved the difference in the first game of the 1964 World Series, which the Cardinals would win in seven games. Shannon never would make an All-Star team, but he became an All-Star teammate. "Mike was the kind of guy that you would want behind you if you went to war," said Bob Gibson, a teammate throughout Shannon's career. "This guy would fight til he died to help you win whatever it was you wanted to win."

As much as Gibson admired Shannon's makeup, he never has been above poking a little fun at the third baseman. Gibson bestowed the "Moonman" nickname on Shannon in 1968 after a batting practice encounter during which one of the players had his mind on more than the baseball field. "We're standing in the outfield at old Busch Stadium, and Mike was looking up at the sky," Gibson said. "That wasn't unusual for Mike, but it was unusual for me. So I got next to him and I looked up and I didn't see anything. I said, 'What are you looking at Mike?' He said, 'I'm looking at the moon.'

"'Why are you looking at the moon?'

He said, 'Let me tell you something, big boy.' He liked to call everyone "big boy." 'One of these days, there's going to be a man walking on the moon.' I went, 'pffft' and walked away. Well, 1969, you know what happened. I started calling him Moonman after that."

The Intimidator—Bob Gibson

Bob Gibson, the greatest pitcher in Cardinals history, was most famous for two things: 1968 and a nasty disposition—not necessarily in that order. Even today, as he approaches 80, Gibson has not lost the tough guy persona. Fans see him at Busch Stadium and quickly make sure he has a clear path. They turn toward each another and talk in hushed tones. *That's Bob Gibson. Better stay out of his way.*

Whether or not Gibson is a meanie doesn't seem to matter. He's had the reputation since the 1950s when one of his professors at Creighton told him he looked angry enough to commit murder. It's too late to shake it now, if he even wanted to. Why would he? To almost be an octogenarian and still be regarded as a badass can't be that bad.

But observe Gibson from a distance these days, and he doesn't appear much different than any senior citizen. We should all be so fortunate to look as fit at that age, and he has not lost the scowl. Get him with some old teammates or put him in front of an audience, though, and you will hear plenty of joking and laughing. Gibson still lives in his hometown, Omaha, Nebraska, but he often travels to Busch Stadium during the season. Just about anytime the Cardinals have an occasion to bring out their Hall of Famers, such as for Opening Day, you can see Gibson wearing his club-issued red suit.

In August of 2014, Gibson even sat down for two 90-minute Q&A

Bob Gibson throws during 1968, a year in which he won the MVP and Cy Young Award and posted a 1.12 ERA.

sessions with a couple of hundred of his closest friends and Cardinals TV announcer Dan McLaughlin. Well, actually, it was a couple of hundred folks who had dished out $225 for dinner and to hear Gibson. But they were regaled with stories that had been shared mostly with friends up to that point.

The topic of 1968 was covered, of course. Known as the year that he changed the rulebook, Gibson posted a record 1.12 ERA, won the MVP and Cy Young awards, pitched 28 complete games (more than any team has pitched since 1991), threw 13 shutouts, and worked 304⅔ innings. Perhaps the most incredible stat from that season is that somehow he lost nine games to go with 22 wins. About his only shortcoming was losing Game 7 of the World Series 4–1 after he had given up one run total in his Games 1 and 4 complete-game victories. "I knew I was bad that year," Gibson recalled. "I was smart as I ever would be, I was as strong as I ever had been, and my control was as good as it ever was. There was a zone that I was in. You usually have it once in a career, and that was the year I had it. It was fun to go out there and know the other team did not want to face me." Above his locker was taped a slogan from one of the popular TV shows of the day that starred Sammy Davis Jr. "Here Comes the Judge," it read, and Gibson certainly ruled that season.

No one could question his dominance that year but what about his disposition? Was he really that nasty or was that as much hype as reality? If anyone in baseball could answer that question, it would be Tim McCarver. He caught 197 of Gibson's starts—more than anyone—and the two remain close friends. So I asked McCarver if Gibson was as mean as we've been led to believe? Perhaps the answer was so obvious, McCarver didn't need to give me a resounding yes. "He hit a lot of guys," McCarver replied.

To be exact, Gibson hit 102 batters over his 17-year career, an average, however, of only six a season. During that span Jim Bunning (136), Don Drysdale (130), and Jim Kaat (111) all plunked more hitters. Gibson never led the National League in hit batsman and finished in the top three only once. He likes to say that most of the guys he hit were asking to be hit. Gibson maintains he was just doing his job, which meant not letting the hitter control both sides of the plate. "The plate is 18 inches across, and if you're standing on one side of the plate and you're looking for a ball on the other side of the plate and the ball comes on this side of the plate, you'll hit yourself," Gibson said. "I would venture to say that 80 percent of the time, guys got hit—not because I was throwing at them but—because they were looking for pitches they didn't get."

One such player was Bill White, a solid left-hitting first baseman who played 13 big league seasons and later became president of the National League. White and Gibson were teammates from 1959–1965 and remain good friends, and Gibson remembers a conversation the two shared during a game when White was with the Cardinals. It was a fairly one-sided conversation. Gibson said he had noticed how much White liked to pull pitches that were outside. Gibson told his friend that if he ever were traded, he better not try that against him. "If you pull that ball that's outside, I'm going to hit you in the elbow," Gibson said.

White replied, "You're crazy."

"No, Bill, I'm serious."

It happened on July 25, 1968. Gibson was facing the Philadelphia Phillies who, like most teams, loaded their lineup with left-handed hitters against him. White came up in the second inning, Gibson threw him a fastball that he estimates was three inches outside, and White somehow pulled it over the first-base dugout. "I went, *aw Bill*," Gibson said. The next pitch? "I hit him right in the elbow." The two went to dinner together after the game, and White questioned Gibson's intent. "Bill, I warned you," Gibson said.

Just as you start to doubt Gibson's fierceness, he makes another point. "I didn't lead the league in hitting anybody but I led the league in scaring the shit out of them." Gibson was just as notorious for how he treated opponents when he wasn't pitching. Even in an era where fraternization was not part of the game, Gibson was known for keeping his

197

distance. The only opponent he says he ever was friendly with was Willie Stargell. "I don't know why, but I liked him," Gibson said.

Even at All-Star Games, Gibson said he did not chum around with his National League teammates, preferring to sit at his locker until everyone had cleared out. "Your job is to beat me, and my job is to beat you. I don't want to be your friend," he said. "When I'm one of your foes, I don't see any sense to have any chitchat when the next day you're going to try to beat my brains out."

Opponents often were intimidated by such behavior, which did not bother Gibson. He learned how to use his reputation to his advantage. "Intimidation is in the eyes of the beholder," Gibson said. "More often than not, people looked at me, and I very seldom smiled. I didn't have a lot to smile about. As I grew up, life was pretty doggone tough. I grew up in the housing projects. I didn't have anything to smile about. Consequently, I grew up not smiling a lot. I really didn't mean to look like that. But when I played baseball, my idea was to win a ballgame, not to win the election. If you're intimidated by me, that was your problem, not mine."

Did that make him mean or just a guy trying to do his job? Remember, in those days, players were competitors trying to earn a living more than entertainers making mega salaries. Gibson says that Sandy Koufax is one of his best friends today, but back then, he had no use for the Dodgers lefty. "He was always beating me 1–0," he said.

Gibson grew up in a housing project in Omaha, where proving his toughness was as much a part of the routine as eating and sleeping. His father died before Gibson was born, but an older brother, Josh Gibson, kept him out of trouble. Gibson says Josh was the neighborhood coach, general manager, and traveling secretary and often rented vans to cart the neighborhood youth all over the state playing baseball and basketball games.

At Omaha Technical High School, Gibson played under a high school basketball coach, Neal Mosser, who he credits with being "instrumental in my learning how to live." A hotshot basketball player, Gibson wanted to play at Indiana. He said Mosser called on his behalf but was told the Hoosiers already had their "quota." "They only had one," Gibson said. "I watched them play and I said they got the wrong one."

So Gibson followed Josh's footsteps and went to Creighton to play basketball and baseball. "I didn't necessarily want to learn anything. I just wanted to play basketball," Gibson said. He did that as well as he played baseball, too. Sixty years after his first season, Gibson's name still can be found in Creighton's basketball record book. His 418 free throws rank fourth all-time, and his 22-point scoring average as a junior remains the program's ninth best single-season mark. Gibson was so good that he even beat the Harlem Globetrotters when they visited Omaha to play a college All-Star team. "I sat on the bench for three quarters. In the fourth quarter, the people started chanting, 'We want Gibson, we want Gibson,'" he said. "They put me in the game, I scored 14 points, and we beat the Globetrotters by one point. After that, they contacted me and asked if I would play with the Globetrotters."

Gibson spent four months with the Globetrotters before turning to the Cardinals full-time. To this day Gibson says he would rather watch a basketball game than a baseball game. "Unless it's a Cardinals game," said Gibson, adding that he better be interested in his former team because he remains on the payroll.

Gibson signed with the Cardinals for less than he was hoping. He knew the Cardinals had signed the McDaniel brothers, Lindy and Von, for $50,000 each and thought he was in their class. "I asked for $35,000 because I knew $50,000 was out of the question," he said. "I didn't know $35,000 was out of the question. I ended up signing for $3,000. Actually, they gave me $4,000 because they gave me a $1,000 [signing] bonus."

Gibson isn't one of those former players who believes the game back then was superior to today. It was different. That's all. "The game has changed. I am not opposed to changes," Gibson said. "That's what's wrong with most of us who are my age. We are so used to doing things a certain way, we don't want changes. Changes are inevitable. You have to adjust. I think I could adjust to it."

Gibson reached the majors two years after he signed and spent the next 17 seasons with St. Louis. According to baseball-reference.com, he never was paid more than $175,000 in a season. For less than $1.5 million in his career, Gibson gave the Cardinals 251 wins, 255 complete games, 3,117 strikeouts, and a 2.91 ERA. He pitched more than 200 innings in a season 12 times, including two seasons with more than 300.

Gibson won an MVP, two Cy Youngs, and nine Gold Gloves; made eight All-Star teams; and saved his best work for October. He won three games in the 1967 World Series against the Boston Red Sox, including Game 7 on three days rest, and he went 2–1 in the 1964 World Series victory against the New York Yankees, including winning Game 7 on two days rest. He was named MVP after both series. He also went 2–1 in 1968's seven-game loss to the Detroit Tigers. In nine World Series starts, Gibson went 7–2 with a 1.89 ERA. As historic as his 1968 was, what he accomplished in 1967 might have been more impressive.

On July 15, in the fourth inning against the Pittsburgh Pirates, Gibson suffered a broken right leg when a line drive hit by Roberto Clemente struck him just above the ankle. Gibson had the leg sprayed with a numbing agent and kept pitching. Three batters later, the bone snapped, and Gibson was thought to be finished for the season. Somehow, 54 days later, he returned to pitch five innings and beat the New York Mets 9–2. The following month, he was the hero of the World Series. "I did not want my arm to go dormant," Gibson said. "I wanted to keep it strong so I threw every day. I came over to the ballpark every day and I would throw. Each day, I would throw a little harder. They took the cast off finally, and in a week or so, I pitched in a ballgame because my arm was strong. My leg was still sore, but I wasn't going to try to outrun anything."

Kissell and The Cardinal Way

On the morning of December 9, 2013, the Hall of Fame held a news conference at the Winter Meetings to announce its newest class would include Tony La Russa, Bobby Cox, and Joe Torre. As the third-, fourth-, and fifth-winningest managers in history, the trio was richly deserving of their newfound baseball immortality. They also were clearly humbled at the honor. When they took their turns at the podium inside the Disney World's Swan and Dolphin Resort, each spent time reflecting on those who had influenced their careers.

If you didn't already realize the impact the late, great George Kissell had made on the game, you certainly had a deeper appreciation after listening to La Russa and Torre. Both skippers praised the longtime Cardinals coach for shaping their careers. La Russa had not managed a game in the majors when he said Kissell gave him the best advice of his career. Torre was equally effusive when he talked about taking over the Cardinals in 1990 and the direction provided by Kissell.

Kissell undoubtedly would have been proud to be recognized by the Cooperstown-bound skippers. But he probably would have felt a little uncomfortable, too. Kissell was not one for the spotlight. His best work was not performed in front of packed stadiums but on the backfields instead. He loved few things more than holding court in the instructional league and teaching youngsters how to play the right way.

His lessons would begin early every morning when the young and the hopeful gathered in a circle to hear about The Cardinal Way. The clubhouse was their classroom, and Kissell was their professor. He would sit on a stool in the middle of the troops and lecture about fundamentals. From fielding ground balls to proper bunting technique to hitting the cutoff man, Kissell would cover every detail and delight in doing so. All he wanted was their attention. All he required was to show up on time.

Kissell had a special way of making sure that tardies were kept to a minimum, too. He kept a box stocked with those old-fashioned, winding alarm clocks, and the first time a young player walked in late, he could expect to be called out. First, Kissell would read the latecomer the riot act. Then he would present him with a gift. He would give them one of his prized clocks. "They weren't late after that," said longtime Cardinals executive Mike Jorgensen, who worked alongside Kissell for years.

Jorgensen knew well of Kissell's love for the game from their time together in the instructional league. Twenty years later, Jorgensen remembered a story that spoke to Kissell's passion. One morning in October of 1993, Kissell was talking cutoffs and relays when he unwittingly found himself on the receiving end of a lesson about a new breed of players. The night before, the Philadelphia Phillies had pulled off a flawless relay play in the National League Championship Series against the Atlanta Braves. Kissell was so impressed with how the Phillies had moved the ball that he brought it up before his players in his clubhouse chat, figuring they had seen the game, too. "He explained this whole play exactly the way it happened, and as he is walking around, he caught a dazed look on a bunch of the kids' faces," Jorgensen recalled. "He said, 'Wait a minute, how many guys watched the game last night?' We probably had 35 kids in the room, and maybe five of them raised their hand. Poor George was heartbroken. He couldn't go on with his lesson for a little while. All day long, he was walking around the diamonds, talking to these kids, trying to make sure they would watch the game that night."

You didn't have to be with the Cardinals to fall under Kissell's influence. Tim Wilken was an up-and-coming scout with the Toronto Blue Jays and was familiar with Kissell and his ways. One fall in the early 1980s, Wilken regularly drove from his home in nearby Dunedin, Florida, to St. Petersburg, then the spring home of the Cardinals, to watch Kissell work during instructional league. Kissell obviously was taking note of the visitors to his yard because one morning he approached the aspiring scout. "You want to come into my office and talk some baseball," Kissell asked after he pulled up in a golf cart that he used to roam the backfields.

Wilken climbed in, and after a few minutes, Kissell asked if he had any questions. Sure, said Wilken, who knew that Kissell had developed a reputation for teaching players how to switch-hit. The Cardinals built much of their success in the 1980s on switch-hitting speedsters, and Kissell would help most of them—Tommy Herr, Vince Coleman, Terry Pendleton, Willie McGee, and even Ozzie Smith.

The key, Kissell explained, was figuring out who could be taught to hit from both sides. To find out, Kissell would take a right-handed hitter, make him bat from the left side, and flip him pitches. After several flips Kissell would toss one firmly at a player's ribs. "If the guy raised his bat and tried to duck away from the pitch, George knew the player didn't have a chance," said Wilken, now an executive with the Chicago Cubs. "But if he kept in his stance and tried to turn on the pitch, George would say, 'He has a chance of being a decent switch-hitter.'"

Kissell reached out to hundreds of players, scouts, and coaches in the 68 years he spent with the Cardinals. He was signed in 1940 out of Watertown, New York, by Branch Rickey but never came close to playing in the majors. But he would go on to work with many Hall of Famers, including two managers. During Torre's playing stint with the Cardinals, he said Kissell taught him how to play third base. When Torre became a manager, Kissell often sat beside him during spring training games and offered basic but essential pointers. "One was he would tell me to look on the field and count the players 1 from 9," Torre said. "Just make sure everybody is out there and where you want them to be. There were a lot of tidbits he gave me that helped show me the way.

La Russa was in his latter days as a player when he was with the Cardinals' Triple A team in New Orleans and was considering whether he wanted to pursue managing as a career or to put his law degree to work. He never has forgotten what Kissell told him. "He asked, 'Do you sincerely love the game and do you have a sincere desire to learn it?'" La Russa said. "'Because they go together,' he said. He told me, unless you really get into learning every aspect of it, you're not cut out for coaching or managing. I was starting to get the bug, and that was a real straightforward way to make a decision." Added La Russa, who would have a chance to spend more time with Kissell 20 years later with the Cardinals, "He was like a father to me, like he was to many."

The late Hall of Fame managers Sparky Anderson and Earl Weaver also credited Kissell with being among their greatest influences. Two other Cardinals greats, Ted Simmons and Tom Herr, are among the many Cardinals greats who have said the same. "Baseball is a game of repetition, and George understood the importance of creating perfect habits through perfect practice," Herr said. "He was great at imparting his knowledge of game situations and the correct way to defend them. He left no stone unturned."

As a 5'8" infielder, Kissell hit .300 in several minor league seasons but only briefly made it to the highest level, Class A, and that was at the age of 31. He turned to coaching in the early 1950s and went on to hold nearly a dozen job titles with the Cardinals—from player/coach to field coordinator for player development—before he died at the age of 88 in 2008 from injuries sustained in a car accident near his home in St. Petersburg. The 68 years Kissell spent with the Cardinals is believed to be the longest time one man has spent with one franchise in baseball.

La Russa said when he was managing the Cardinals, rarely would a day pass during spring training when players and coaches from the opposing team did not stop by and visit with Kissell. "The number of people who would come around and give him a hug or talk to him was amazing," La Russa said. "He touched as many lives as anybody who's ever been in uniform in this game."

Kissell is considered the father of The Cardinal Way, the timeless manuscript for playing the game the right way. At 73, in 1993, Kissell won a lifetime accomplishment award from minor league baseball. Two years later, the Cardinals named the franchise's annual award for player development after him and made him the first winner. A decade after that, the team put Kissell's name on the Roger Dean clubhouse at their spring training base in Jupiter, Florida, along with a plaque that reads, "Every player in the Cardinals' Organization since 1940 has had contact with George Kissell and they have all been better for it."

George liked to think he was an old-school tough guy, but he was moved to tears at the ceremony. He would have had another reason to get a lump in his throat if he could have heard two of his former students talk about him on the doorsteps of the Hall of Fame.

Stan the Man's Royal Send-Off

Stanley Frank Musial was the best of St. Louis. He moved to Missouri when he made the Cardinals in 1941 as a 20-year-old and never left. He embodied the Midwestern ideal: friendly, humble, decent in the best sense of the word. Musial is regarded by all accounts as the greatest Cardinal and was considered by those who knew him an even better man.

From the night of his death on January 19, 2013, until he was buried a week later, Musial was given the send-off befitting a man who had meant so much for a region. After years of declining health, he died at his home in the St. Louis suburb of Ladue on a Saturday evening at 5:45 pm. Much of his family was at his side.

Within the hour TV and radio stations all over the area had interrupted their programming with the news. The *St. Louis Post-Dispatch* put out a 14-page commemorative section that was in newsstands by the end of the night. Five days later thousands withstood freezing temperatures to wait in line to attend a public visitation held in the historic Cathedral Basilica. Coverage of Musial's funeral service held inside the near-capacity Basilica was carried on local television stations. Hundreds gathered at the Musial third-base statue at Busch Stadium to witness the funeral procession's wreath-laying ceremony. As the procession prepared to depart, the crowd spontaneously broke out in "Take Me Out to the Ballgame," a tune often played by Musial on his always-handy harmonica.

Bob Costas, who began his storied announcing career in St. Louis and lived for many years there, gave the main eulogy. He was a longtime friend of Musial and his family. After stopping to check his emotions several times, he shared personable stories about Musial the man. Costas talked about the weekend Mickey Mantle stayed with him during a trying period before Mantle stopped drinking. Costas and his wife were hosting a dinner and—to make Mantle more comfortable—they invited Musial and his wife, Lil. Mantle told Costas that he would not have a drink all day or night out of respect for Stan. "I don't want to do anything foolish when Stan is here," Mantle told him.

After all the guests had left and midnight approached, Costas was sitting with Mantle. At Musial's eulogy, Costas shared what he called an intensely honest story that said much about Mantle and Musial. Mantle told him: "You know I had as much ability as Stan, maybe more. Nobody had more power than me, nobody could run any faster than me. But Stan was a better player than me because he was a better man than me. He got everything out of his life and his ability that he could. He'll never have to live with all the regret that I lived with."

When Mantle died a few years later in 1995, Costas performed his eulogy. Costas said the services were vastly different. While Musial's was largely a celebration of his life, Mantle's had been a far sadder affair because of all the regret and sadness during his life. Mantle died at 63 from cancer—not long after undergoing a liver transplant that was needed because of his years of alcohol abuse. Costas said when he was eulogizing Mantle, he would glance at the VIP section in the church and see so many great Yankees and other New York athletes and celebrities. But at one point, Costas said he looked up, and against the wall, far from the dignitaries was Musial. "In that moment, I was struck by the sheer decency of that simple act," Costas said. "Nobody would have marked Stan Musial absent that day. He never played with Mickey except in All-Star Games, never played against him, wasn't in the same league, wasn't linked with him like Willie Mays was. No one would have marked him absent. It struck me in that split second that a 74-year-old man, who had battled prostate cancer, had gotten out of bed that morning, had gone to Lambert [Field], gotten on a flight by himself, and had flown out with no special treatment to pay his respects to a man, who respected him so much, to try and comfort a family that was in a great deal of pain."

In another anecdote, Costas talked about how his daughter, Taylor, became childhood friends with one of Musial's granddaughters, Lindsay. Early in the friendship, when the girls were six or seven, Taylor came home and told her parents that Lindsay had said she could come over any night of the week except Saturday and that her friends could go over to her house on Saturdays. On Saturday nights, Lindsay had to stay home because her grandpa delivered McDonald's on Sunday morning. "And so a seven or eight-year-old girl would come home," Costas remembered. "And you'd say, well, what did you do? 'We stayed up late, we had a pillow fight, we played video games, and then in the morning, Stan the Man brought us Egg McMuffins.'"

Just about everyone who had the good fortune of meeting Musial has a favorite story. Bob Gibson, with a reputation for being about as nasty as Musial was nice, has often told the story of being a rookie when Musial was in the latter stages of his career. Because Gibson wasn't pitching much that season, he said he often stayed out late after games and would be dragging the next day. "I would come to the ballpark tired and go sit down in the corner of the dugout," Gibson said, relaying the story during a speaking engagement in 2014. "We had this great big dugout in old Busch Stadium. I remember sitting there one day and I was just gone, snoring. Stan came down and said, 'Hey kid, hey kid. Come on, game's over.' He woke me up so nobody would catch me. I thought that was really nice. He could have just left me there. Stan was really, really a nice individual. If you didn't like him, I had to go and check you out because there's definitely something wrong with you."

The great Mays remembered how he had been treated by Musial at an All-Star Game in the late 1950s, a time when black players still were treated as outcasts by many major leaguers. As told by Royals Hall of Fame radio announcer Denny Matthews, Mays said a group of black and Latin players were playing poker by themselves in the back of the clubhouse when Musial walked up and told them to deal him in. "And Stan didn't know how to play poker," Mays said. "But that was his way of welcoming us, of making us feel a part of it. I never forgot that. We never forgot that."

George Vecsey, columnist for *The New York Times*, who authored a best-selling autography about Musial, wrote about how much he liked "a family man who put up his own Christmas lights on his ranch house in a modest neighborhood." Wrote Vecsey: "A friend of mine recalled going to a department store and seeing Stan and Lil testing the mattresses, bouncing up and down. They were regular citizens in a town that prized approachability."

After being traded to the Los Angeles Angels, hometown St. Louis hero David Freese started wearing No. 6 in honor of Musial. Freese told me that one of his most cherished possessions is a baseball card with a photograph of him on one half and Musial on the other. "I was signing a bunch of cards [after Musial's death], and all of a sudden, they pulled out 25 cards of Stan and me," Freese said. "A face shot of him and a face shot of me with him at the top with his signature, me on the bottom with my signature. They told me that was the last thing he ever signed. I was like wow."

Long before Mike Matheny played for the Cardinals—much less managed them—he came to St. Louis for a wedding in 1991. Matheny had been drafted by the Milwaukee Brewers a few weeks earlier, but somehow Musial found out who he was because he befriended him at the reception. "Stan was there with Jack Buck," Matheny recalled. "Stan came over on his own, talked to me, and 30 minutes later, he's still treating me like I was something special. I couldn't believe it. It was unforgettable." The wedding party, Matheny said, had booked a popular musical group, but the band saw the stage for one song. "Stan took the rest of the time," Matheny said. "Nobody was about to ask him to get off the stage."

Bud Selig even exercised his executive powers on behalf of Musial. In 1999, MasterCard and Major League Baseball asked fans to vote for the greatest 100 players of all time, and the top 10 outfielders would be considered part of the starting lineup. Musial, as sometimes happened, was overlooked by the fans and finished 11th among outfielders. Selig considered that such an injustice that he formed a special committee to make sure the makeup of the team was as accurate as possible. Musial ended up in the starting lineup at the expense of none other than Roberto Clemente.

For all the accolades and attention that Musial received, his career still is considered underrated. He did not play in New York like Joe DiMaggio and he did not hit .400 or win two Triple Crowns like Ted Williams. He did not hit as many home runs as Henry Aaron or play with the flair of Mays. Musial reached the World Series three times, but the last was in 1946, the year before the World Series was televised for the first time.

But look at the Man's numbers, and a convincing case can be made that he was as great as any player this side of Babe Ruth. Musial hit .300 in each of his first 16 seasons, finishing his 22-year career with a .331/.417/.559 slash line. He owned more than two dozen National League records when he retired in 1963, including most games (3,026), runs (1,949), RBIs (1,951), extra-base hits (1,377), and hits (3,630). His 475 homers were second to Mel Ott's 511. Musial's hits, remarkably, were divided equally with 1,815 at home and on the road.

The always congenial Stan Musial, who played 22 years for the Cardinals, assumes a batting stance in 1951.

He is the only player to win three Most Valuable Player awards while starting at a different position (first base, right field, and center field). Four times Musial led the National League in doubles *and* triples. In 1948, at 27, he came within a home run of winning the Triple Crown, finishing with a .376 batting average, 131 RBIs, and 39 homers.

Musial hit three homers in a game when he was 41 years old and finished with a .330 batting average in 135 games that same season. He walked more than he struck out in every season except his last, ending his career with 1,599 walks to 696 strikeouts. He never struck out more than 46 times in a season in 1953 and he walked 105 times while whiffing only 32. And he missed what would have been one of the prime seasons of his career, 1945, when he went into the Navy during World War II.

No one signed more autographs more graciously than the Man. Legend has it that he kept the trunk of his car stuffed with baseball cards, baseballs, and other items that he regularly signed and handed out. After his buddy, John Wayne, told him he wouldn't have to sign matchbooks if he kept his own cards with him, Musial regularly pulled out a signed picture of himself to give away. On those rare occasions when nothing else was available to sign, he would take a dollar bill and not only autograph it, but also turn it into a ring in a way where you were sure to see the signature.

Kathy DeWitt, the wife of Cardinals chairman Bill DeWitt Jr., told the *St. Louis Post-Dispatch* that she still has a few dollar bill rings folded up by Musial. Dan Dierdorf, the pro football Hall of Famer, told the newspaper that his wife keeps her dollar-bill rings in her jewelry box "because they're priceless."

It's almost like if you have lived in St. Louis for long and don't own a Musial autograph, you feel left out. By the time I moved to St. Louis, Musial's health had started to fail and his appearances at Busch Stadium were becoming more limited. I can remember him once in Busch Stadium pulling out his harmonica on the elevator ride from the press box to the field and playing "Take Me Out to the Ballgame." One of his friends later told me that was one of only two songs he could play. "Happy Birthday" was the other.

I have a Musial autograph that I count among my prized possessions. In the early 2000s, my then-wife was having lunch with her boss in the same restaurant where Musial was dining. Her boss knew Musial well enough to introduce her. "My husband is named after you," she told him.

"Anyone who is named after me gets a bat," he said matter-of-factly.

Her brush with fame made a nice story at dinner that night but soon was forgotten. Until a couple of weeks later when a delivery truck pulled up to our house, and out came a cardboard package that looked like a three-foot long shoebox. Inside was pure Adirondack ash. No receipt, no note. Neither was needed. The inscription on the bat said everything:

"To Stan McNeal,

"My namesake—

(signed) Stan Musial, HOF69."

Usually when I tell that story in St. Louis, someone relates their own story about a meeting with the Man. I know from the gleam in their eyes how much it means to them. My parents grew up in Florida and never lived anywhere close to St. Louis. But even during the 1940s and '50s, before TV and computers, Musial's fame stretched to my dad's home in Lakeland, Florida. He spent many afternoons at the Boys Club arguing with a buddy over who was greater—Musial or Williams. Eventually, they came to a sound conclusion: Williams was the better hitter, Musial the better ball-player. "He was my idol," my dad told me the night that Musial died.

Cardinals Red

The night before Stan Musial died, Red Schoendienst was feted with a 90th birthday party at Mike Shannon's restaurant in downtown St. Louis. Red's birthday wasn't until February 2, but with a number of Cardinals greats in town for the Winter Warm-Up, the time seemed right to celebrate Red. In the days that followed Musial's death, it was difficult not to think about Red, his longtime teammate and close friend. Musial's passing was one of the biggest stories of the year in St. Louis, as well it should have been. But I kept thinking, I hope Red receives a send-off just about this grand, too.

If you believe bringing up death is insensitive when talking about someone in their 90s, accept my apology. I hope that Red is roaming around Busch Stadium for many more years. When he passes, though, I hope he is given the farewell he deserves. Red has meant as much to the Cardinals as Musial. Except for a four-and-a-half year stretch near the end of his playing days, Red has been a part of the Cardinals organization since he signed as a 19-year-old out of a tryout camp at Sportsman's Park before spring training in 1942.

In the 73 years since, Schoendienst incredibly has been a player, manager, or coach on 11 Cardinals teams that have reached the World Series. He owns six championship rings with St. Louis, more than anyone in the organization. As a Hall of Fame player, Schoendienst was a slightly undersized, switch-hitting second baseman with good wheels, a slick glove, and a live bat. He spent 15 of his 19 seasons as a player with the Cardinals and made 10 All-Star teams, hit .289, and was selected to the Hall of Fame in 1989 by the veterans committee.

Until Tony La Russa came along, Schoendienst also had managed the Cardinals to more wins and for more games than anyone in club history. He guided the Cardinals to the World Series championship in 1967 and the National League pennant in 1968. He was hired as manager less than two years after his retirement as a player and held the job for 12 seasons until he was fired following a 72–90 campaign in 1976.

The rags-to-riches story of Albert Fred Schoendienst makes quite a history lesson. Born 40 miles east of St. Louis in tiny Germantown, Illinois, he grew up in a home that did not have electricity until he was 10 years old. He joined the Civilian Conservation Corps as soon as he was old enough to secure a social security card. He was signed by the Cardinals after hitching a ride to a tryout camp in St. Louis on a dairy truck with a couple of buddies. Though Red left without a contract, he signed a day later when the Cardinals' head scout returned to town and wondered what had happened to the skinny, freckle-faced redhead.

A mishap on a CCC job almost cost Red his left eye before he earned his first $75 monthly paycheck as a ballplayer. On his last day in the minors before leaving for a year in the service, he ran into a wall and messed up his shoulder, an injury that bothers him to this day. "The only treatment I got was fighting snakes and gators in Florida," he said about training camp. Years later, toward the end of his career, Red overcame a bout with tuberculosis that cost him all but five games of the 1959 season. "I played with a sore arm and practically one eye my whole life," he said.

Red came up with the Cardinals in 1945 and played left field, a vacant position when Musial spent a year in the military. The Cardinals won the 1946 World Series in his second season, and with Musial back, Red moved to second base and played next to Marty Marion for five straight seasons. Marion is a man Red calls the greatest shortstop he has ever seen and, yes, that includes the Hall of Famer Ozzie Smith.

Branch Rickey, the Cardinals general manager at the time, watched Red's first game in the minor leagues and, despite two errors, told the 19-year-old that he would make a fine player. Red was playing shortstop for the Rochester (New York) Red Wings when Walter Alston was the first baseman. No, he didn't have an idea that Alston would become a great manager. "We were thinking about playing," he said.

He roomed with Musial on the road and rode with him to the ballpark when the Cardinals played at home. He was a teammate of Willie Mays with the New York Giants, helped Hank Aaron win a World Series with the Milwaukee Braves in 1957, and once was traded for Bobby Thomson of the Giants. He coached under Johnny Keane, Whitey Herzog, and Joe Torre and served as a spring training instructor for La Russa. He managed numerous Hall of Famers, including Bob Gibson, Lou Brock, Orlando Cepeda, Steve Carlton, and Torre. "Red is such a good, honest to goodness baseball guy, I have felt very blessed to be around him," Torre said. "When I managed the Cardinals, he was on the bench, and while bench coach wasn't an official title, he was mine. He was there for me during the games. When I played under him, he was a lead-by-example guy. He'd keep you in line, but he knew that you already knew how to play the game. He was definitely an influence on me."

These days, Red still can be found at Busch Stadium when the Cardinals play at home. Sometimes he puts on his uniform—donned with the retired No. 2—and heads out to talk with the players during batting practice. He's spending more of his time in the cooler climes of the clubhouse area these days, where he will get a massage, eat dinner in the players' lunch room, and head upstairs to watch the game from a suite.

To have a chance to sit down with him and talk about "them days" is a treat as much as an education. Understandably for someone who has seen thousands of players, he's not easily impressed. Ozzie Smith was a "good shortstop." Jackie Robinson was a "good ballplayer, a good athlete. Mr. Rickey was smart enough to pick the right man." Musial, of course, was "a helluva ballplayer, just a good solid player, a natural."

As Torre says, Red wasn't much for bells and whistles, as you can tell when he talks about his time in the game. On batting practice: "We didn't have much batting practice because we didn't have many baseballs. We might have a dozen for a batting practice. You'd only get a few swings. A visiting club would come in and get maybe get 20 minutes to hit. There were no batting cages for them either."

On playing so many day games: "It was like a 9 to 5 job almost. I liked it, but them old ballparks were hard to see in because of the shadows and everything. At Wrigley Field people sat in center field so there was no hitting background whatsoever. A lot of parks didn't have one. At Sportsman's Park, we did have a pretty good background because they wouldn't let anyone sit out there. But there were always shadows because of the time we played."

On attendance at Cardinals games in the 1940s and '50s: "Weekends we drew real good because we played doubleheaders on Sundays. We would have a lot of people coming from all over because people would come for the whole weekend. We'd have a game on Friday night, an afternoon game on Saturday, and then a doubleheader on Sunday. We'd even draw from North Carolina because the Cardinals had so many minor league teams in those areas. People would follow players from the minors til they got here. Tennessee was big here, and Arkansas, of course, because of the Dean boys."

On what happened when a player didn't hustle: "Terry Moore was the captain and he'd get on you pretty heavy. If someone didn't run a ball out, he'd be waiting when they came in the dugout. He'd grab you right on the shoulder and give you a pinch. 'You're fooling with my money,' he'd say. The only way we could make money is if we got in the World Series and though it wasn't much, it was something, and you wouldn't have to go to work that quick in the offseason."

On what the Cardinals players earned for winning the World Series in 1946: "After taxes, and taxes weren't that much in them days, we wound up with about $2,700. Marty Marion, our shortstop, didn't think that was right. He called a meeting with the rest of us and talked about it. We all threw in $50 to pay the lawyer to try to get it going. Our club didn't take much convincing, but it was real tough getting some of the other clubs. Pittsburgh was a big union town with all the steel mills and they made it tough on the Pirates players. But Dixie Walker with the Dodgers and Early Wynn with Cleveland were real gung ho and they helped get a movement for more pay going. But Marty Marion was the real one behind it."

On his experience working with the CCC: "We'd build dams, fences, government things. Got a dollar a day and stayed in those old-time barracks. It was a good program. Your day was full. You had to do this and you had to do that. You saluted the flag every morning and every night when you came in. It was all about discipline, and I'd like to see that today."

Red candidly admits that the daily routine of being at the ballpark around ballplayers helps keep him feeling useful into his 90s. "That's why I feel pretty lucky they still let me come out," he told *Cardinals Gameday Magazine*, "not that I do that much. I'm here with the ballplayers. I'm in the clubhouse. I love to sit around with these young guys. It keeps me going."

ACKNOWLEDGMENTS

Without the help and support of many, I probably still would be seeking deadline extensions and wondering when this project would be completed. I owe a big thanks to my contacts at Triumph Books, Jeff Fedotin and Noah Amstadter, for their flexibility and patience during my times of stress.

Likewise, thanks to the editors at my day job, Mike Nahrstedt and Jase Bandelow, for working with me and understanding only so many words can be written in a day.

Thanks also to all the fine folks who call the Busch Stadium press box their office from April through October. Being around this crew is entertaining as well as informative.

For my money no newspaper in the country covers their hometown team in any sport better than the *St. Louis Post-Dispatch* covers the Cardinals. Derrick Goold, Rick Hummel, Joe Strauss, Bernie Miklasz, and Tom Timmerman get the good stories because they ask the right questions. I have learned plenty from them.

I have learned just as much watching Cardinals telecasts on Fox Sports Midwest. Whether Dan McLaughlin is flanked by Rick Horton, Al Hrabosky, or Tim McCarver, the broadcasts always are entertaining.

Rob Rains also has taught me much and deserves extra thanks for helping me land this project.

R.B. Fallstrom, Brian Stull, Jenifer Langosch, David Wilhelm, J.J. Bailey, Calvin May, Joe Williams, and Bob Nightengale all make going to the ballpark more enjoyable. So do Brian Bartow, Melody Yount, and Chris Tunno of the Cardinals media relations team.

Thanks also to Fallstrom for the freelance work he sent my way during the 2013 season. If it had not been for R.B., I would have missed the all-nighter at Busch Stadium on May 30 (and June 1), 2013, which still is one of my most memorable Cardinals games.

I appreciate the good guys at *Cardinals Gameday Magazine*—Jim Gilstrap, Tom Klein, Gabe Kiley, and the boss, Steve Zesch—for giving me the opportunity to contribute to their publication. Some of that work has filtered into these pages.

My son, Jackson, deserves a pat on the back for being the first eyes on many of the words here and providing helpful feedback. He is one of the biggest Cardinals fans around so when I was able to tell him something he didn't know, I knew I had a good passage for the book. Thanks also to my youngest daughter, Kate, for her proofreading efforts and feedback. Like a true aspiring journalist, when Kate said a story was good, I knew she was not just saying it.

And, finally, thanks to Colleen, my wonderful wife, for her support and belief in me.

SOURCES

The vast majority of the quotes used in this book came from one-on-one interviews and press conferences that I attended in clubhouses, dugouts, manager offices, and media rooms. In addition to my notes and observations, I studied several books and scoured numerous websites in my research. One recurring lesson: you could fill a library with all the great material that has been written about the Cardinals.

Among the most helpful sources:

St. Louis Post-Dispatch and stltoday.com

Mlb.com, particularly its excellent backlog of box scores, play-by-plays, and pitch-by-pitches

Retrosheet.org

Baseball-reference.com

Fangraphs.com

Baseballhall.org

Cardinals Gameday Magazine

BOOKS

Tony La Russa and Rick Hummel—*One Last Strike: Fifty Years in Baseball, Ten and a Half Games Back, and One Final Championship Season*; Harper Collins Publishers, New York, 2012.

Derrick Goold—*100 Things Cardinal Fans Should Know and Do Before They Die*; Triumph Books, Chicago, 2010.

Red Schoendienst and Rob Rains—*Red A Baseball Life*; Sagamore Publishing, Urbana, Ill., 1998.

Rob Rains—*Cardinal Nation*; Sporting News, St. Louis, Mo., 2006.

Matthew Leach—*Game of My Life: St. Louis Cardinals*; Sports Publishing, New York, 2011.

Buzz Bissinger—*Three Nights in August: Strategy, Heartbreak, and Joy Inside the Mind of a Manager*, Houghton Mifflin Harcourt, Boston, 2006.

David Halberstam—*October 1964*; Fawcett Books, New York, 1995.